INDIA THROUGH A BISHOP'S DIARY

INDIA THROUGH A BISHOP'S DIARY

OR

MEMORIES OF AN INDIAN DIOCESE
- - BY ITS FIRST BISHOP - -

BY

EYRE CHATTERTON, D.D.
First Bishop of Nagpur

LONDON
SOCIETY FOR PROMOTING
CHRISTIAN KNOWLEDGE
NORTHUMBERLAND AVENUE, W.C. 2
1935

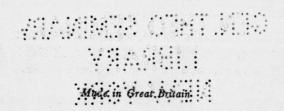

Made in Great Britain.

TO MY WIFE

CONTENTS

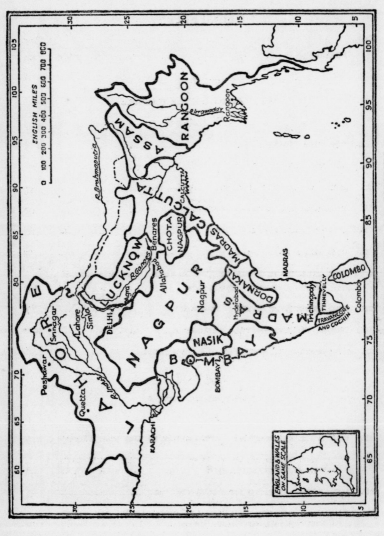

A MAP OF INDIA SHOWING THE DIOCESES

(Reproduced by permission of the Press and Publications Board, Church Assembly.)

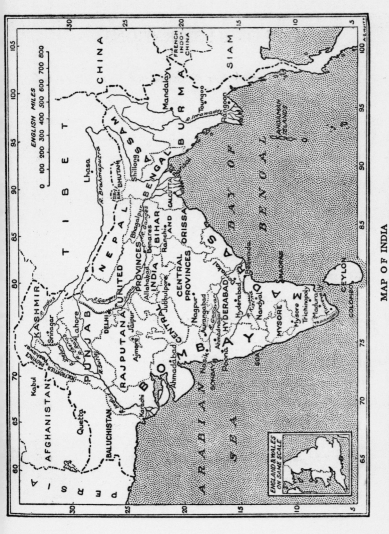

MAP OF INDIA

(*Reproduced by permission of the Press and Publications Board, Church Assembly.*)

LIST OF ILLUSTRATIONS

FOREWORD

THE India of my diary is not the India which everybody knows and everybody goes to see. It is not the India of great cities like Calcutta, Bombay, and Madras which owe their existence to the British. It is not the India of the rice fields of Bengal or of the tea gardens of Assam. It is not the India of the long and rather dull Ganges Valley, or of the dry and dusty Punjab where the virile Mohammedan and Sikh people reside. It is not the India where mild and gentle Tamils and Telugus live. It is the India of Native States and splendid upland jungles. Here Indian Princes and their subjects still live very much as their ancestors did. Here some millions of the primitive aborigines of India live peacefully away from the haunts of the politician. Here the proud Rajput fought for his independence against the Mughal and here the British saved these brave Rajputs from the Mahratta. Here—so the Metropolitan of India told me on the day when he committed this great region to my spiritual care—lies two-thirds of the romance of Indian history.

EYRE CHATTERTON,
Bishop.

PART I
1903—1914

THE MAKING OF THE DIOCESE

CHAPTER I

THE NEW DIOCESE

The New Diocese of Nagpur—Consecration of its first Bishop—Its three great territories—Gondwana—The old Gond Kingdoms—Lingo, the Gond prophet—Mahratta rule—The Battle of Sitabaldi—Pindaris and Thugs —The modern Central Provinces—Native States of Central India— Rajputana—The Land of Princes.

EDWARD RALPH JOHNSON, fourth Metropolitan of India, 1886—98, was a Bishop with a statesman-like vision. During his twenty-one years' Episcopate he took a leading part in the creation of no less than six Indian Bishoprics—Lahore, Rangoon, Tinnevelly, Travancore, Lucknow, and Chota Nagpur. It had become increasingly clear to him for some years before his resignation that the huge central regions of India, stretching almost from sea to sea, needed far more personal supervision than any Bishop of Calcutta, however young and vigorous, could possibly give them, and so for some years before he left India he had begun to lay the foundations for another Bishopric in the Central Provinces of India. Bishop Wilkinson, then Bishop of North and Central India, had again come forward to help with the endowment of the new Bishopric as he had already done in the case of several of the other Indian Bishoprics. The loss of his two brothers in the Indian Mutiny, it is said, had stirred him deeply to help the Church of India in every way he could.

When Bishop Johnson's successor, Bishop Welldon, arrived in India, the consent of the Government of India to the creation of this new Bishopric had already been obtained, and they had agreed to attach to it the salary of a senior chaplain, as they had done already for the Bishoprics of Lahore, Rangoon and Lucknow. They did so with the understanding that the Church would raise endowments for these Bishoprics which would yield an equivalent sum. The attitude of the Indian Government in thus giving financial help to these Bishoprics was decided by the fact that one of the important duties of

3

these Bishops was to supervise the work of their Government chaplains in their care of the British troops and other British officials.

The sum needed for the endowment of the Central Provinces' Bishopric was raised fairly quickly—Bishop Welldon himself being a large contributor, and it would have fallen to his lot to consecrate the first Bishop of Nagpur had not serious illness compelled him to leave India without hope of return. His withdrawal was a heavy blow to the Church as his great educational experience as Headmaster of two great English Public Schools might have enabled him to carry on still further the remarkable work which his predecessor, Bishop Cotton, had done for our Church Schools in India. The duty of consecrating the writer as first Bishop of Nagpur fell therefore upon his successor, Bishop Reginald Copleston, a distinguished oriental scholar, who before his translation to Calcutta had been for twenty-seven years Bishop of Colombo. The consecration took place in St. Paul's Cathedral, Calcutta, on March 25th, 1903, when Bishop Copleston, Metropolitan of India, was assisted by Bishop Clifford of Lucknow and Bishop Whitley of Chota Nagpur.

The Diocese of Nagpur is certainly a peculiar one. It embraces within its limits three large territories, each of them almost the size of England and Wales. If India were not unified under one central government these territories would be described as three separate and very different countries. Within them many languages are spoken—Hindi, Urdu, Mahratti, Telugu, Gujerati, Uriya, Bhili, and Gondi. The Diocese, as will be seen by a glance at a map, from its widespread position, touches at one point or another most of the larger and three of the smaller Indian Dioceses. Of its three territories, the Central Provinces is the only one in British India. The two other territories, Central India and Rajputana, are large groups of native feudatory states under their own Indian Maharajahs. While the history of Central India and Rajputana is well known, thanks to writers like Sir James Malcolm and Colonel Tod, it is far otherwise with the Central Provinces. Apart from a fascinating description of it in

Forsyth's old-world book " The Highlands of Central India,"
and detached pieces of history to be found in Government
District Gazetteers, little or nothing is known save by those
who have lived there.

It was spoken of in the Middle Ages by the Mohammedan
Chroniclers as Gondwana—the land of the Gonds. These
Gonds were a large race of aboriginal Dravidian people who
had moved up from Southern India, and had settled in this
country. The famous chronicler, Abu-l-Fazl, of Mughal
days, makes certain caustic remarks about them which are
worth quoting : " In the vast territories of Hindustan there is
a country called Gondwana. It is a land inhabited by the
tribe of Gonds ; a numerous race of people, who dwell in the
wilds, spend their time in eating and drinking and in the
procreation of children. They are a very low race and are
held in contempt by the people of Hindustan, who look on
them as outcast from their religion and their laws. In former
times there was no supreme ruler in Gondwana, but the
country was ruled by several Rajahs or Rais, and at the
present time, when by the will of fortune it belongs to this
race, there are several Rajahs. The fighting men of this
country are chiefly infantry—horsemen being few. From the
earliest establishment of the Mohammedan power in India
no monarch has been able to reduce the fortresses of this
country or annex its territory."

Twelve years after my consecration, having read all I could
find about these Gond rulers and people in District Gazetteers
and other Government publications, and having visited their
fortresses and palaces as well as the charming city of Chanda,
I felt drawn to weave together all I had learnt of these four
Gond kingdoms in a book called " The Story of Gondwana."
There are at least two things in the story which deserve some
mention. Cut off as these regions are from Northern India
by rivers and inaccessible forests, teeming with wild animals,
it is clear that adventurers, Rajput and Mohammedan, from
time to time, entered them, and were welcomed by the Gond
chieftains and intermarried with their daughters. Learning in
this way of the higher civilisation of Northern India and

Rajputana, these Gond rulers were seized with a not unworthy ambition of defending their countries and developing their kingdoms along more civilised lines. No one can visit the old Gond fortresses, Chauragarh in northern Gondwana, Deogarh and Kherla in central Gondwana, and Chanda the former capital of southern Gondwana, without seeing the same kind of Saracenic architecture as is to be seen in the Mohammedan cities of Northern India. To their simple courts came Brahmin pandits who cast horoscopes at the birth of their children, and supplied them with wonderful pedigrees such as the pedigree of Hirde Shah, on a tablet at the Palace of Ramnagar, which describes the heroism of his ancestors in language that baffles translators. Some of these Gond rulers achieved a fame outside their own jungle kingdoms. It is stated that the Moghul Emperor Akbar visited Jatba, the Rajah of Deogarh, and that later Jatba visited Delhi. One of Jatba's descendants, Bakht Buland, for a time held some post at the court of Delhi under the Emperor Aurungzeb, and received from the Mughal his name of Bakht Buland—" one of great Respect." Judging, too, from the majority of the names of these Gond aboriginal princes, it seems clear that there was considerable Mohammedan influence in Gondwana.

Most famous of all was Durgavati, the Gond Queen of northern Gondwana. This Boadicea of ancient Gondwana died in battle. Mounted upon her elephant, she fell when leading her army fearlessly against the Mohammedan invaders of her country. Her simple tomb, called by the villagers the "Chabutera," ten miles from Jubbulpore, is still held in reverence by all who live in that neighbourhood, and simple votive offerings are to be seen strewn all over it. A poem by "Pekin" concludes with these lines:

> "The Kingdom of the Gonds is gone,
> But noble memories remain,
> And with a loving awe we scan
> The battle page which ends thy reign, Durgavati!"

But perhaps of even deeper interest than the old Gond Kingdoms are the quaint Gond songs which link themselves round the name of their ancient and mysterious prophet and teacher, Lingo. These songs were first brought to light by the Rev. Stephen Hyslop, a distinguished pioneer missionary of the Scottish Free Church. They were songs of the Gond Pardhans (or bards), and were sung by the Gonds at their wedding festivals and on other joyous occasions. Taken down by Hyslop most carefully in Gondi, they were afterwards translated into Hindi and turned into English blank verse by that versatile genius, Sir Richard Temple, the first Chief Commissioner of the Central Provinces. The story of Lingo is published in full in Sir Richard Temple's translation.[1] It has all the charm of Longfellow's " Hiawatha."

Let me outline this song-cycle very briefly :

" By the decree of the High God Bhagawan, Lingo was born of the flower of a tree called Dati. ' Without father or mother,' this teacher and civiliser of the Gond race came into being. Lingo was a perfect being. ' Water may be stained, but he had no stain whatever.' The helpless infant was fed by honey which dropped into his mouth from a fig tree. He spent his childhood Pan-like in the absolute solitude of the jungles. He came to his maturity rapidly. He felt his loneliness and craved for the society of men like himself. The Gond race at this time, all save four persons, had been incarcerated in a mountain by the God Mahadeo. Their wild and filthy habits had enraged Mahadeo, and he had lured all save four into this mountain prison. Lingo met these four Gonds and became their teacher. He taught them an easy but wasteful form of cultivation, the Dhaya. He showed them how to produce fire from flint, and he hunted with them. He left them for a while, and returned having found wives for them. The wives admired Lingo more than their husbands. Lingo was angry and thrashed them. The story resembles Joseph's temptation. The four Gonds were jealous and killed their teacher. The High God produced a nectar which, sprinkled on Lingo's body, restored him to life. He was full of forgiveness for his murderers, and determined to go to the rescue of the imprisoned race of Gonds. To do this

---

[1] Much of it will also be found in my " Story of Gondwana," illustrated by Miss Alice Woodward.

he had to undergo severe penance for a whole year, and having in this way acquired immense merit, the God Mahadeo acceded to his request and released the captives. Lingo then divided the Gonds into various tribes or classes, and taught them about the various gods. He divided the tribes still further into families, which consisted of those who worshipped seven, six, five, or four gods. Those who worshipped seven gods must not marry within their own seven-god family, but must wed in one of the other three families. He taught them quaint ceremonies in worship, and bade them keep faith with their Totem the tortoise (which they certainly have not done). His task at length accomplished, he bade them look yonder to the gods, whither he himself departed. They cried, ' Where is our Lingo gone? ' "

There is much to charm one in this old-world child-like story with its sympathy with the beauties of the jungle, and in the humour of those who take part in its little dramas. It has a deeper side, too, as it invited the Gonds to think that they owed their simple civilisation to a being of a higher order than themselves. Lingo was a perfect man. " Water may be stained, but no stain had Lingo." He rejected temptation, he forgave his murderers and forgot their ingratitude, he rescued the Gond race, and then passed on to the gods. Was not this strange mythical personage in some way preparing these primitive people for the message of the Gospel?

Then after four centuries of rather primitive and happy rule under their four Gond Rajahs, the country passed under the sway of Mahratta rulers. Their first conqueror, the Bhonsla Rajah of Berar, was the descendant of one of Sivaji's distinguished cavalry leaders. The Mahratta was a soldier, rather than an administrator, fighting was the main business of his life; his rule was oppressive to a high degree. Gondi ceased to be spoken and Mahratti took its place. The Gonds withdrew into the jungle countries of Chanda, Bastar and the Satpuras, and Mahratta cultivators of the Khumbi caste took their place.

In the middle of the eighteenth century the East India Company first entered into treaty relations with the Mahrattas, who were then aiming at complete ascendancy in India; and in 1798 our first British resident, Mr. Colebrooke, was appointed to reside at the court of the Bhonsla. Mr. Colebrooke saw all around him a country plunged in misery, an unpaid Mahratta army often turning itself into bands of armed dacoits who looted the country far and wide. The farmers " sowed in sorrow with little hope of reaping; when they did reap, they buried their corn in the ground." Things moved from bad to worse until in 1817 the Bhonsla ruler Mudhoji, in combination with other chieftains of the Mahratta Confederacy, the Peshwa at Poona and Scindhia at Gwalior, determined to stamp out for ever British rule and influence in India. Few in England to-day have ever heard of the Battle of Sitabaldi Hill at Nagpur, where on November 26th, 1817, a small body of British officers with only 1,800 Madras Infantry, 300 Bengal Cavalry and four guns withstood for long hours the onslaught of the Mahratta army, which numbered 18,000 infantry, of whom 4,000 were Arabs, and 36 guns. Never was almost certain defeat turned into magnificent victory, solely by the courage of one man, Captain Fitzgerald, of the Bengal Lancers. The Fort of Sitabaldi was on the point of falling when Captain Fitzgerald, in defiance of the orders of his superior officer, charged at the head of his cavalry, completely surprising and routing the Mahratta Cavalry, and capturing several of their guns. This successful piece of daring (" he had charged at the hazard of his commission," so Grant Duff tells us) put such courage into the soldiers in the Fort that they charged down the hill, put the enemy to flight, and captured most of their guns. Certainly, among deeds which won the Empire, Captain Fitzgerald's daring charge on November 26th, 1817, should never be forgotten.

After this act of treachery and violence, the Mahratta ruler, Mudhoji, was deprived of his rule in the northern part of the Central Provinces, in what was called the Saugor and Nerbudda territories, but was allowed to continue his rule under close supervision in the southern regions. Then when fresh intrigues with the Peshwa at Poona were discovered, he was deposed, and his grandson, a child, was recognised as Rajah. When in 1853 he died without issue, the administration of the whole of the Central Provinces was taken over by the British. To-day the descendant of the old Gond Rajahs of Deogarh, deprived of his rule by the Mahrattas, and the descendant of the Mahratta Bhonsla, Rajah of Nagpur, deposed by the British for misrule, live peaceably and in apparent contentment at Nagpur, as pensioners of the Government of India.

Our first British rulers in Gondwana had no easy task when they entered into the heritage of Mahratta misrule. One of the first questions which the Provisional government had to face in 1817 in northern Gondwana was whether widows should be sold for the benefit of the state, and whether persons selling their daughters should not still be taxed one fourth of the price realised! The country was still suffering from the wandering bands of robbers called Pindaris, who from their standing camps in the Nerbudda valley swept over the country carrying fire and sword, death and destruction, wherever they went. Those who would know the truth about the Pindaris must turn to Malcolm's " Memoirs of Central India."

Nor does this complete the tale of woes which pervaded the Central Provinces at that time. There is in Christ Church, our civilian Church in Jubbulpore, a memorial tablet to Colonel Sir William Sleeman, who was sent by government on special duty to suppress " Thuggism," that highly elaborate system of religious murder which had spread over large tracts of North and Central India at this evil period of crime and violence. These human fiends, having made their acts of worship to Kali, Goddess of Blood, would associate themselves with unsuspecting bands of travellers, and having shared with them their evening meal, would, without the least compunction, strangle them. Between 1826 and 1835, 1,562 Thugs were tried by Sir W. Sleeman at Jubbulpore, of whom 1,404 were hanged or transported for life. Some of them confessed to over 200, and one to 719, murders! Some of these Thugs, deprived of their means of livelihood, were provided for by the paternal government in a settlement at Jubbulpore.

Before describing how Gondwana, now the central Provinces, has fared under its British rulers, it will be well to give some description of the country itself. Like Caesar's Gaul, it divides itself into three parts, the country south of the Satpuras, the Satpura hill-country, and the country to the north of it. The country to the south of the Satpuras is of the northern Deccan type. The climate is hot and rather dry. It has large and fertile plains in Chhattisgarh and Berar, fine forests in Chanda, and wild and rather hilly country in the Bustar State. The Berar is a great cotton growing country; its jinning factories and cotton mills support a numerous and industrious people. Of recent years an increasing quantity of its cotton is going to Japan. There is considerable mineral wealth in this part of the Central Provinces, both coal and manganese iron. Nagpur, the capital of the Central Provinces, lies in this region.

The Central region or Satpura country, with its ranges of lofty hills or mountains, and its wide-stretching plateaux, is one of the most attractive regions in India. Within its hills rise some of India's great rivers, the sacred Nerbudda—a southern rival of the Ganges, the Tapti with its rocky bed, the Sone, the Mahanadi and the Wainganga. Within its huge forests rove tiger, panther, buffalo, wolf, elephant, antelope, and the wild boar. There is no region in India more popular than the Central Provinces with lovers of big-game shooting. Here, too, are sacred places, Amarkantak, the source of the Nerbudda, the cave of Mahadeo in the Pachmarhi hills, the temple of Mandhatta with the dread Birkila rock in the Nerbudda, the temples of Ramtek twenty-five miles north of Nagpur, the temples of Vishnu and his ten incarnations on the Wainganga, as well as numerous shrines on hill-tops and by river-sides, to which pilgrims in their thousands journey every year, seeking Mukti or salvation.

The northern portion of the Central Provinces, nearly 200 miles north of Nagpur, is a far cooler and more pleasant region from the European point of view. Its principal city, Jubbulpore, lies in the Nerbudda valley between the Satpura and Vindhyan mountains and hills. How pleasantly situated it is and how charming is the surrounding country will be evident from the fact that at one time it was seriously considered whether it might not be the headquarters of the Government of India. While rice is widely cultivated in the southern part of the Central Provinces, wheat is widely cultivated in the Nerbudda valley. In the southern parts of the Central Provinces Mahratta influence predominates, and Mahratti is the official language. In the northern area Hindustani is the official language, the majority of the people being Hindus rather of the north India type. The Mohammedan population is neither large nor influential. Over two million Gonds, who speak their own language, live in the Satpura jungles and hill-country.

If in the earlier days of British rule the Central Provinces were in a backward state, it is certainly so no longer. The time has passed when the office of Chief Commissioner of the Central Provinces was regarded as but a stepping stone to some higher official position in India, and when many a Chief Commissioner, after passing most of his service in some other Province, remained for too short a time in the Central Provinces to enable him really to understand its problems. To-day its Governors are generally selected from members of the India Civil Service who have served most of their time in this part of India, and know the people intimately. As to-day they have to carry on the government of the Province with an elected legislative Council, it will easily be seen how important it is that they should know fairly well both the country and the people with whom they have to deal. Many of the Chief Commissioners of the Central Provinces have in the past distinguished themselves as Lieutenant Governors in other Indian Provinces, but if we are to select any of the number who should always be remembered for what they did while Chief Commissioners of the Central Provinces, we would mention the names of Sir Richard Temple, first Chief Commissioner, and Sir Reginald Craddock.

To Sir Richard Temple was entrusted the laying of the foundations of our rule in this territory, which he did both wisely and well. By raising the status of a number of the leading zamindars, or landlords (some of them of the Gond race), to the rank of petty Rajahs, he secured their loyalty and encouraged them to develop the resources of their states, and to care for the welfare of their people.

To Sir Reginald Craddock we owe to a large extent the modern civil-station of Nagpur. Those who remember, as the writer does, the Nagpur of thirty years ago, appreciate this as a modern visitor cannot do. Laid out on a wide and spacious plan, its new and handsome Government buildings, the new suitable residences for its officials, its improved water supply, and later on, its Legislative Council Hall, its University buildings, and its fine modern railway station, have now made it what it never was before, a really fitting headquarters of the Government of the Province. If I have dealt rather fully on this part of the diocese it is because no important part of India is so little known to the outside world.

When we enter Central India we pass into an entirely different atmosphere. No longer are we under British rule, but have passed into the kingdoms of the Indian Princes. Central India is the official term for a large group of Indian feudatory states. It lies to the north of the Central Provinces. This territory is under the general supervision of a distinguished British official who bears the rather lengthy title of Agent to the Governor-General in Central India. Working under him are a small body of British officials, recruited either from the Indian Civil Service or the Indian Army, who are located at the headquarters of the principal Indian princes. The Headquarters of the A.G.G. are at Indore, and his duties are many and his powers considerable. He is the chief adviser of all the Indian Princes in the area, and is their guardian during their minority. He exercises the functions of a Court of Appeal, and is the natural medium of communication between the Princes and the Imperial Government. The British officials working under him are styled Residents in the larger states, and Political Agents in the smaller. This Central India territory lies between three important rivers, the Nerbudda on the south, the Chambal on the west, and the Ganges on the north and east. It is fertile and well cultivated, especially in the Malwa area, and has fine jungle and hilly country in the Bundelkhand and Bhagelkhand areas. There is considerable mineral wealth in Central India—iron, coal, and even copper. There are, as one might expect, a considerable number of aboriginal people, Gonds and Bhils, in its wild and more hilly parts. Its two largest states are Gwalior and Indore. Their rulers are descended from famous generals in the Mahratta armies. The Maharajah Scindia of Gwalior with a state larger than Wales has an army of about 12,000 troops of all arms, and the Maharajah Holker of Indore with very extensive territories has an army of about 9,000. Both of these armies take a share in the Indian Imperial Defence Force.

Those who would understand how the offshoots of Rajputana's princely houses in times past built up kingdoms in Central India at places such as Orchha, Panna, Chitarpur, Rewah, Nagode and elsewhere, should read Sir John Malcolm's famous " Memoirs of Central India." Though Central India is mainly peopled by Hindus (Rajput and Mahratta), there is one quite important Mohammedan state, that of Bhopal, south of Gwalior, whose rulers, especially the late Begum, have taken a leading part in Indian affairs of recent years. There is also the small Mohammedan state of Jaora north of Indore.

There are places of great historical interest in Central India. The famous Buddhist " tope " at Sanchi, near Bhopal, which is raised over some " bone of the Founder Gautama," and the ruined shrine at Bharhut, near Sutna (some of whose carved remains are in the Museum, Calcutta), were places of special sanctity in ancient India. Thither Buddhist pilgrims in their thousands came to venerate the " stupas " where lay portions of the founder's body. The magnificent ruined city of Mandu, which overhangs the northern side of the Nerbudda valley, is to my mind one of the most impressive places in all India. Beginning as the seat of a Mughal Viceroy, it became later the capital of a small Mohammedan kingdom. Here, as in many other places in India, the late Lord Curzon, when Viceroy of India, prevailed on its ruler, the Mahratta chieftain of Dhar, to restore some of its most important buildings.

It has been the long-continued policy of the Central Government of India, by suggestion and when requested by co-operation, to endeavour to help the rulers of these States to improve the condition of their people. One notable instance of this is to be seen at Indore, where an important college for sons of native chiefs and nobles, bearing the name of " Daly College " after Sir Henry Daly, a former Agent to the Governor-General, is doing very valuable work in training the future rulers and nobles of Central India. Here a few picked English University men, with an Indian staff, have a unique opportunity of educating and bringing excellent influence to bear on those who have to play an important part in India's future.

Leaving Central India we now pass into Rajputana, the third, and from a historical point of view, by far the most important part of the Nagpur Diocese. Like Central India, it is a group of native states, twenty in number, and many of them of great prestige. In the centre of this great country with its sandy, barren plains, and its numerous fertile valleys and oases, cut across as it is by the Aravalli range of mountains, with their red sandstone rocks, lies the small British district of Ajmeer Merwara, where are the headquarters of the Agent to the Governor-General, whose functions in this region are much the same as those of the A.G.G. in Central India. He, too, has under his direction a number of British officials, who reside at the various headquarters or courts of the Indian Princes. This country takes its name of Rajputana from its ruling race, the Rajputs, a proud aristocracy who have furnished ruling dynasties in many of the native states of India. From the earliest days of the Mohammedan invasions of India, the Rajputs have fought with reckless bravery for their independence. At the end of the sixteenth until the early part of the eighteenth century, they were compelled to acknowledge the suzerainty of the Mughal Emperors at Delhi. With the rise of Mahratta power they fell on evil days until their independence was restored to them by the British, and they became our firm allies. Later on I shall be speaking rather fully of Ajmeer and of the more important of the native states, which it was my privilege and duty to visit for many years, and where I invariably received the greatest kindness and consideration.

Those who would really desire to know the history of this romantic part of India, the various clans and tribes of its people, and their strange and ancient customs, need only turn to Colonel Tod's monumental history called " The Annals of Rajasthan." It was in Rajputana, and especially in the state of Mewar, whose capital at Udaipur has been called the Venice of the East, that Colonel Tod spent long years of his Indian service, and amassed the enormous amount of information which is to be found in his famous book. In Miss Gabrielle Festing's " Land of Princes," we get a most readable and charming account of parts of Rajputana; and Rudyard Kipling in " From Sea to Sea " has given us interesting pictures of famous places such as Jodhpur, Jaipur, Bikanir and Chita, in his own peculiar and brilliant style. It was in these central regions of India that my work was to be for twenty-three years. The work was full of interest, and the land was full of romance.

CHAPTER II

EARLY DAYS. 1903—7

Enthronement in All Saints' Church, Nagpur—First Headquarters in Jubbulpore—The Hill Station of Pachmarhi—Visit to Bishop Lefroy in Simla—Attend Synod of Bishops in Calcutta—My First Visitation of Clergy—My First Ordination—Our Second Diocesan Conference, 1906—The Formation of a Diocesan Board—A Visit to England for six months—Formation of Nagpur Diocesan Association—Interview with Mr. G. F. Bodley about Cathedral—The Metropolitan's Visitation of the Diocese.

ON the day before my consecration I had a kind invitation to lunch with Lord Curzon, then Viceroy of India. I remember his saying to me when I was leaving, " It is an interesting thing to be the first Bishop of a new Diocese," and when I said something about the responsibility of early decisions which my successors might regret, he at once looked at me and said, " Responsibility is the very breath of life." I think these words of his impressed me all the more because I was compelled to make some early decisions on my own responsibility with which some persons whom I highly respected did not at the time agree.

Let me endeavour to picture my Diocese as it then presented itself to me. It was a huge tract of country, three times as big as England and Wales, more than 1,000 miles from east to west, and more than 600 miles from north to south. It had mission districts, military cantonments and civilian stations dotted about it, separated by great distances. There were fair-sized European and Anglo-Indian centres like Nagpur, Jubbulpore and Ajmeer; there were between sixty and seventy small communities of English and Anglo-Indians, many of them connected with railways, the majority in the Central Provinces; there were six missionary centres, three in the Central Provinces, and three in Rajputana; there were seven military stations with British troops, three in the Central Provinces at Jubbulpore, Kamptee and Saugor; three in Central India at Mhow, Neemuch and Nowgong; and one in Rajputana at Nasirabad. The Central School of Musketry for the Army was at Pachmarhi, the gun carriage factory at Jubbulpore, and, later on, the Cavalry School at Saugor. Besides these larger military stations, there were at Agar and Guna, in the Gwalior state, two regiments of the historic Central India Horse; at Kherwara in Rajputana, the Mewar Bhil Corps; at Ajmeer, the Ajmeer-Merwara Battalion; at Deoli, an Indian regiment; and at Indore there was still another regiment, the Malwa Bhil Corps.

How was one to draw these scattered heterogeneous communities into the life of the new Diocese, and make them feel that they were a living part of it? Obviously my first duty was to go round and see them all as soon as possible, and let them see what sort of person their new Bishop was!

The hot weather was coming on rapidly when I reached Nagpur early in April. There I received a very kind welcome. My enthronement took place on the evening of April 5th in All Saints' Church, Nagpur. As the temperature was then between 110 and 112 degrees, most of the senior officials and their wives were away in Pachmarhi, our hill station, or on leave in England. The ceremony of enthronement was carried out by the senior Chaplain, the Rev. G. M. Davies, who shortly afterwards became my first Archdeacon. The throne was a handsome chair of stained Indian teak and the massive pastoral staff was a fine piece of Indian silversmiths' work. Both these were gifts of my clergy and faithful laity. The pastoral staff was so massive and so heavy that Bishop Whitehead remarked that it looked as if it was intended to crush rather than to lead my flock! Later on my wife presented me with a beautiful light pastoral staff which went with me everywhere, even on my three visits to our troops in Mesopotamia.

All Saints' Church was at that time the size of an ordinary country Church in England. It could seat about 230 people. It was admirably situated in fine grounds, or a " compound " as we call it in India; it had a nice stone tower and pretty groined verandahs. How the genius of the late Mr. G. F. Bodley transformed it into our little Cathedral will be told later on. One interesting old figure amongst the few clergy who were present was the Rev. Dr. Fraser, father of Sir Andrew Fraser, Lieut.-Governor of Bengal, and grandfather of the Rev. Alexander Gordon Fraser, C.B.E., the distinguished Principal of the famous African College at Achimota, Gold Coast, Africa. Dr. Fraser was at that time ninety years of age. He had been in India for sixty years without leaving it. Originally a Presbyterian, as were his forefathers, he had been ordained by Bishop Johnson twelve years before. In spite of his advanced age he thought nothing of long night journeys to visit his out-stations, and generally preached for forty minutes!

After spending ten days in Nagpur, with a visit to Kamptee, our most southern military station, I started off on my first visitation tour, which included visits to Chanda, the head-quarters of the Scottish Episcopal Mission; Mhow, our largest military station, and Indore, the headquarters of the Agent to the Governor-General for Central India. I reached Jubbulpore towards the end of April, when travelling had become very trying owing to the rapidly increasing heat. Until my own " hired home " was ready, for I had decided for the time being to make my headquarters at Jubbulpore, I and my Chaplain, the Rev. G. E. M. Tonge, were the guests of the Commissioner and his wife, Mr. and Mrs. Fox-Strangways, at the Residency. I owe a great deal to their kindness in those very early days.

My first visitor at Jubbulpore was the Rev. Charles Hope Gill, afterwards Bishop of Travancore, who came over from Allahabad to discuss with me the handing over of the secre-taryship of the C.M.S. Missions in my Diocese to one of our Nagpur C.M.S. missionaries. The selection of the Rev. Herbert J. Molony, who had been for many years at work amongst the Gonds in the Mandla District, was made to the satisfaction of everyone. When four years later Herbert Molony was taken from us to succeed Bishop Moule as Bishop of Chekiang in China, it is no exaggeration to say that the whole Church of the Central Provinces mourned. Our chief consolation was that India's loss was China's gain. I should add that the office of secretary in our C.M.S. Missions is an

C

admirable testing and training for a missionary Bishopric. He
has to be a father and mother to a number of missionaries
and their wives and even children. He has to see to all their
needs—pay, allowances, holidays, furlough, bungalows, touring equipment, etc. He has to arrange for the language study
and examination of young missionaries. He is expected to
visit the different missions in his area, and to report to his
society. He works under an Advisory body called the Cor-
responding Committee, on which certain of the missionaries,
selected chaplains and sympathetic laymen generally sit with
the Bishop of the Diocese. This Committee, of which he is
Secretary, corresponds directly with the Home Committee of
the C.M.S. in London. Your ideal secretary must be a sound
man of business, thoughtful and sympathetic, and a spiritual
tonic to his brother and sister missionaries.

The first appointment which I actually had to make was
that of an Archdeacon. Under Government ruling I had to
select my Archdeacon from the " cadre " of Government
Chaplains, and for obvious reasons. In the first place he had
to take charge of the Diocese in the Bishop's absence, and in
his hands were placed the care and the oversight of Government Churches and cemeteries. He was expected to know all
Government rules on such matters, and to be able to advise his
brother Chaplains on matters of furlough pay, travelling
allowances, and office management. My choice fell on the
Rev. G. M. Davies, the senior Chaplain of the Diocese, and I
knew the Diocese was well satisfied with the choice.

From the middle of May till the " Monsoon " rains broke,
the hottest period of the Indian year, I stayed in Pachmarhi.
Here I made the acquaintance of the Chief Commissioner, the
Honourable Mr. J. P. Hewitt (afterwards Sir J. Hewitt,
Lieutenant-Governor of the United Provinces), and the leading
officials of the Central Provinces. Mr. Hewitt had been in
Calcutta for my consecration, and during the short time he
remained in the Central Provinces he was always ready to help
me when he could.

I have often wondered what the Central Provinces would
be without Pachmarhi, our beautiful little hill-station in the

WATERS MEET, PACHMARHI, C.P.

Satpuras! As a hill-station it goes back to the days of Sir Richard Temple, first Chief Commissioner. Knowing the temperature of Nagpur could be somewhere between 112 and 118 degrees in the hot weather months, he sent out search parties to explore the Satpuras for a suitable place to which he and his administrative officers could retire for the hot weather; they found it at Pachmarhi. On the southern side of the Nerbudda valley lies this beautiful park-like plateau at an elevation of 3,500 feet, flanked on the south and west by three fine mountains which are about 4,500 feet high. The plateau is beautifully timbered and has a circumference of about ten miles. Between the plateau and the three mountains, Chauragarh, Mahadeo and Dhupgarh, are really magnificent gorges with a narrow river of lovely clear water running between high cliffs. Here one finds long stretches of cool, deep water where one can swim in the heat of an Indian summer day secure from the fierce rays of the sun.

During my time as Bishop of Nagpur I generally spent from six weeks to two months every year at Pachmarhi. My plan was to invite one of our missionaries or some junior assistant Chaplain to be my guest for this period, and to assist me at the Church services and other spiritual work in the station. It was good for them and their wives, if married, to get away from their rather out of the way districts into a cool climate with pleasant society, and they were able to interest many people in their work. We had quite a gem of a Church in Pachmarhi, the work of a Mr. Irwin, a well known architect, who made use of the local stone in a most effective way. Twice during these twenty-three years we made additions to it according to the architect's design: first by building a transept, and after the war by building the tower. The tower was built as a thanksgiving for our victory, and in the appeal for funds I alluded to the famous Jai Stambh, or Tower of Victory, at Chitor Rajputana. Towards its erection one or two of our leading Hindu gentlemen subscribed generously, and on one day in Pachmarhi we raised nearly £200 for it. After my marriage in 1910, the Vicarage was always crowded in the hot weather, as my wife had a genius for making everyone welcome and happy. One recalls delightful visits from members of the Oxford Mission in Calcutta, our dear friends Father Brown, Father Strong and Father Ralph Drake Brockman, and from Canon, now Bishop, Wood, Canon J. R. and Mrs. Mackenzie, the Rev. R. Hack, the Rev. Kenneth Mackenzie, M.D., M.C., D.S.O., and many others.

The mixture of civilian and military life made Pachmarhi additionally pleasant. Every year numbers of young British officers came up for their musketry course. There was every kind of healthy recreation, polo, riding, walks and climbs, swimming, golf and tennis. For me, too, it was a time for reading, writing and planning. The hospitality was most generous and pleasant.

Shortly after my return to Jubbulpore at the commencement of the rainy season, I paid a fortnight's visit to Bishop Lefroy in Simla. He was then Bishop of Lahore and later on became Metropolitan of India. The special object of my visit was to consult the Viceroy about the question of making my headquarters at Jubbulpore instead of at Nagpur, the capital of the Central Provinces. I was desirous of doing so for several strong reasons, and had spoken to the Metropolitan of India of my wish to do so. After some conversation with Lord Curzon, and at his request with Sir Denzil Ibbetson, then Home member of the Viceroy's Council and previously Chief Commissioner of the Central Provinces, I obtained their assurance that they could see no objection to my so doing, and fully agreed with me in thinking that it was more central to the Diocese as a whole, and a far more invigorating and pleasant place to live in.

One very special reason, however, which made me prefer it to Nagpur at that time was the opportunity it gave me, when not on tour, of taking an active part in the missionary work which was being carried on in Jubbulpore and surrounding villages by the Church Missionary Society, and the Church of England Zenana Missionary Society. I had spent seven years when Head of the Dublin University Mission to Chota Nagpur in acquiring a goodish knowledge of Hindi. I had been in the habit of preaching and speaking in that language for years.

Here was a golden opportunity of using it. It must be remembered that at that time our Church had no missionary work in Nagpur, and the language in that area was Mahratti, which I had not studied. And so from 1903 till the end of 1907, when not on almost perpetual tours, I made my home at Jubbulpore; nor shall I ever regret it. The place itself is, in my opinion, the nicest plain station in India, a little bit of old England in the heart of that great country. There certainly was much to attract one in Jubbulpore. One could get plenty of tennis, golf and riding in a very pretty country. One could have a day's fishing on the Nerbudda at the Marble Rocks where the Mahseer (Indian salmon) were not always obliging. There was plenty of pleasant English society, military and civilian at the Club, and a very nice company of English missionaries connected with the C.M.S. and C.E.Z.M.S. I could preach any Sunday either to British troops or civilians, or at the Mission Church, a pleasing variety. And yet before five years had passed I felt clearly that I must make my headquarters and home in Nagpur. Not that my fondness for Jubbulpore ever changed, nor had the reasons which first drew me to it altered; what really happened was that I saw that the real and permanent influence in the Central Provinces lay in Nagpur, the headquarters of Government, and that nothing would ever be done to strengthen and develop Church life there if the Bishop of the Diocese did not throw in his lot with those who lived there.

Before returning to my Diocese I had a delightful week's walking tour with Bishop Lefroy in the hill country behind Simla. We spent a Sunday at Kotgarh C.M.S. Mission Station above the Sutlej valley, a lovely and most restful spot for an " old missionary." Lefroy was a keen mountaineer. I can still picture him striding along with his hat in one hand and an Alpenstock in the other. On one occasion he surprised two bears in a low fruit tree. One of them charged him on the narrow mountain path and, missing him by inches, went over the hillside, a miraculous escape! I must have been very much the " Interrogative Bore " on the expedition, for I am quite sure I asked the Bishop nearly every question I could about the workings of an Indian Diocese.

On my return to my Diocese I began at once a series of tours which lasted almost without ceasing for the next ten months. I used to say that I travelled 10,000 miles in my first year! From the end of July till Christmas I aimed at visiting as many stations as possible in the Central Provinces, reserving Central India and Rajputana for the cold weather months after Christmas. In a good many places candidates were ready for confirmation. I spent some time in Nagpur and shortly before Christmas again visited the Scottish Episcopal Mission at Chanda when I consecrated S. Andrew's, the Mission Church, using the Scottish Communion office, translated into Mahratti, at the request of the Missionaries. Shortly after Christmas I spent a fortnight in the Gond Mission with Herbert Molony and my Chaplain. We rode about 150 miles across the jungles, staying at Patpara and Marpha, its two most important centres. This was the first of many, almost annual, visits to this interesting mission, but the only one in which I had the companionship of Herbert Molony. It was the first time any Bishop had travelled right through the district and visited all its mission stations. We had a little thrill one morning as we were told that a man-eating tiger was on the prowl close to us! We had to dismount from our horses and have our rifles ready. We luckily escaped, but he got his victim the following morning. The man-eating tigers have often been very troublesome in several parts of the Central Provinces, and from time to time officials who are expert shots have been put on official duty to exterminate such pests. I remember how one man-eating tiger in Chota Nagpur killed 270 people before he was shot!

From the wilds of the Gond Mission I journeyed straight to Calcutta to attend the Synod of Bishops. This was my third visit to Calcutta during the first year of my episcopate. It was a very interesting experience, as it meant meeting all our Indian Bishops for the first time in council. We were presided over by Bishop Copleston, then Metropolitan of India. Bishop Valpy Franch, the first Bishop of Lahore, used to be called by the natives of the Punjab "the seven-tongued man of Lahore," but Bishop Copleston quite surpassed him in this respect as it was said he could speak thirteen languages! He was consecrated Bishop of Colombo when only thirty years of age, and after twenty-seven years in his island Diocese was made Bishop of Calcutta and Metropolitan of India. He held that office for ten years more. He was a great Oriental scholar. The late Bishop Gore told me that he considered Bishop Copleston's book on " The Buddhism of Magadha " was one of the finest books on the Buddhist religion. I feel of him as I do about Bishop Johnson, that some worthy record of the work he did in the East should have been written years ago.

At this my first Synod my dear old friend Bishop Whitley was present for the last time. He had been brutally assaulted a short time before by some drunken natives who had mistaken him for a cooley recruiter! As he entered the Palace Library where our Synod was meeting, with his head bandaged, everyone rose in deep respect. He served the Church in India for over forty years, first as a missionary, and then as a Bishop. To him was entrusted by Bishop Milman the delicate task of guiding the old German Lutheran missionaries in Chota Nagpur, when they and many of their Kol converts joined the Anglican Communion.

After the Synod I journeyed to Rajputana, where I spent over a month visiting important places—Ajmeer, Nasirabad, Jaipur, Bandikui and Phalera as well as the C.M.S. Mission at Bharatpur, and also the fascinating C.M.S. Mission to the Bhils. At most of these places I held confirmations. One is sometimes inclined to think that interest rather diminishes when one visits places frequently, but I have never felt this about my almost annual visits to Rajputana. There is a subtle and old-world charm about the native states of India and their people which one finds nowhere else. Who that has seen the pink city of Jaipur, or travelled across the desert to see Bikanir rising like an island out of the sea, or seen camels and elephants jostling through the narrow streets of Jodhpur, or gazed from the Residency at Ajmeer on one side at the lake, and on the other at the picturesque city lying between Taragarh and another hill, can ever forget them?

Just a year after my consecration nearly all the clergy of the

Diocese came to Jubbulpore for my first visitation. Our first day was spent as a Quiet Day in prayer and meditation. On this occasion I felt drawn to give the three addresses, though in after years I generally invited one of the Oxford Mission, or of some other brotherhood, to do so. In my visitation charge on the second day I dwelt, as might be expected, almost entirely with the problems of our own Diocese. On our third day we had two most interesting discussions. Our morning subject, especially for chaplains, was " How best to interest the laity in the work of the Church "; our afternoon subject, especially for missionaries, was " How best to present the Gospel to Hindus and Mohammedans." At this conference we started our Diocesan Quarterly Magazine which has done so much to draw all our scattered Christian Communities together and to create a real Diocesan feeling. Our first editor, the Rev. Barclay Kitchin, did his work admirably. He turned a deaf ear to the suggestion of a monthly paper, knowing how difficult it would be even once a quarter to get really interesting material. I regarded it as part of my duty to write a very full letter in the magazine every quarter to let the Diocese know what we were doing and hoping to do.

In May 1904 I held my first ordination. It was a small one, only two English priests, and one Indian deacon. The question of increasing the number of our clergy was clearly of immense importance. There were in my Diocese at this time only twenty-four English priests, one Cingalese priest for our Tamil congregation at Nagpur and no Indian.

I held my first three ordinations in Christ Church, Jubbulpore. For my first ordination the Rev. C. Hope Gill helped us greatly by some excellent addresses at the Quiet Day preceding the ordination. After moving my headquarters to Nagpur in 1908, I always ordained our priests in the Cathedral of All Saints', though at the special request of missionaries I ordained several deacons in the remoter districts where they were to work, so that their Indian converts might have an opportunity of witnessing the solemn service. On looking over past records I find that during my Episcopate I held twenty ordinations, and ordained forty clergy, of whom seventeen were Indians. What a contrast to the huge ordinations of our Home Bishops! In 1910 the number of our clergy had increased to forty-seven, but with the unhappy reduction of our English missionaries the number is now about forty-two.

I was very fortunate in securing really good examining Chaplains. In India we expect all Europeans whom we ordain, chiefly missionaries who come out either as laymen or deacons, as well as our Indian Clergy, to know something of the principal tenets of the Hindu and Mohammedan religions.

In the autumn of 1904 I went up for a few days to Chota Nagpur, where I had begun my missionary work in India twelve years before. It was a farewell visit to Bishop Whitley, though I did not then know it, for in less than two months he had finished his course, and entered into his well-earned rest. Almost his last words to me were that looking back on his forty years in India, " he felt that goodness and mercy had followed him all the days of his life." I was delighted to see how well that Dublin University Mission was getting on. Things had moved forward splendidly. I was specially struck by the new College, St. Columba's, so largely the creation of that most indefatigable of missionaries, the Rev. James Arthur Murray. I was present at one of their debates. There is nothing which an Indian student loves more than a debate in which his subtle intellect can find free play.

After leaving Hazaribagh in Chota Nagpur, my Chaplain and I were joined by the Rev. Herbert Molony, and we journeyed together for a month's walking tour in Kashmir. I had visited Kashmir ten years before with a dear friend, Father Brown of the Oxford Mission to Calcutta, so that it was not altogether a new experience. Before going there in 1894 I had read very carefully Moore's famous poem of Lalla Rookh, " Who has not heard of the Vale of Kashmir," and I had often wondered, and still wonder, how the poet could have filled that enchanting valley with such an atmosphere of romance without ever seeing it. He had buried himself, so one reads, in some farm house in Derbyshire, and filled his mind with pictures of its beauty and of Mughal stories of romance. We had a delightful month. Of course we visited

Tyndale Biscoe's famous school, and even took part in one of
the rowing races in its school regatta. We also visited the
Neve's C.M.S. Hospital and lived for a fortnight on a rather
primitive doonga, or houseboat. One splendid day stands out
in one's memory when, at the head of the Liddar Valley, we
had a stiff and venturesome climb up and across the great
Kolahoi glacier with its snow mountain of 17,000 feet towering
above us.

Again in the autumn of 1905 I journeyed to the Himalayas
for the purpose of visiting Ranikhet, a favourite military
hill-station which had been assigned to my Diocese under an
agreement between the Bishops of Calcutta and Lucknow. As
the Chaplains in my Diocese, before it was cut off from the
Calcutta Diocese, could always look forward to two years of
their service in a Himalayan hill-station, which is almost as
cool as England, it was not considered fair to deprive them of
their privilege, and so for the time it was decided to make
Ranikhet our Nagpur Diocesan hill-station. I was anxious
to visit it that I might form some idea of what it was like for
the work of our Chaplains. My Chaplain and I spent two or
three pleasant days in Naini Tal with the Bishop of Lucknow
and Mrs. Clifford, and having secured useful hill ponies
journeyed over to Ranikhet.

Next to Darjeeling, it is certainly the most beautiful hill-
station I have seen. Its snow giants, Nanda Devi and
Trishul, the former 25,000 feet and the highest mountain in
the British Empire, are a constant joy and inspiration to gaze
upon. " I will lift up mine eyes unto the hills from whence
cometh my help." I suppose the Psalmist's hills were Tabor
or Mount Hermon, and if they could have inspired this godly
man with thoughts of God's greatness, what should not the
Himalayas do! After wandering for three weeks in the
Kumaoun country, fishing its main river unsuccessfully, and
visiting the Pindari glacier, we returned to India. On my
return journey I conducted the Annual Retreat of the Cambridge Mission and the S.P.G. Brotherhood at Cawnpore. A
month later, at the invitation of Bishop Lefroy, I conducted
a Retreat for his clergy at Lahore.

The next event of real importance in the early life of the Diocese took place in 1906, when at our second Diocesan Conference we inaugurated a Diocesan Board which was to deal with questions of education in our schools, especially religious education of the young, the development of our missionary work, the increase of our chaplaincies, the building of Churches, and the raising and disposing of moneys for our work. We had prepared very carefully for the formation of this Board. Our leading stations with their out-stations were entitled to send duly elected lay representatives. For those stations which were too remote to send representatives, owing to heavy travelling expenses, we selected persons to represent them who lived near Nagpur, and who knew something of their area, and who would be able to attend. I should add that this Board continued to carry on the work for which it was created for ten years until, during the period when Bishop Lefroy was Metropolitan, the Episcopal Synod decided on a fully developed system of Diocesan Councils, with a Central Provincial Council in Calcutta. This was done as a preparatory step to the Church in India's becoming a self-governing body, which took place after protracted negotiations both within the Church itself and with Government in 1930.

On the occasion of our second Diocesan Conference Bishop Clifford came over from Allahabad and conducted a Quiet Day which we all deeply appreciated. In him I always found a most kind and helpful friend and adviser.

By this time it had been decided that the Cathedral of the Diocese was to be at Nagpur, and that All Saints' Church was to be duly enlarged and become our Cathedral. Steps had also been taken to build a suitable house for the Archdeacon, close to the Cathedral. We had taken as our model for this house, the residence of the senior Chaplain at Allahabad, close to its Cathedral. I was still uncertain about when I should transfer my headquarters to Nagpur, though I had been offered by Sir Reginald Craddock a very nice site for a Bishop's house near the Central Provinces Club at Nagpur, which I accepted.

In 1906 I paid a six months' visit to England. I wanted a little rest after three years of almost perpetual touring, but above all I wanted financial help to carry out what I now saw was absolutely needed for the work of our Diocese. My old friend and commissary, Canon W. Bartlett, then Vicar of St. Barnabas, Sutton, had taken an immense amount of trouble to find openings for me in various places. I cannot altogether say it was a restful holiday, but I know it was a very useful one as regards arousing interest and getting help for the Diocese. One of the most important bits of work which we carried through during this visit was the starting of our Association for the Nagpur Diocese. It was affiliated from the first with the Indian Church Aid Association. Several important parishes where I was known, formed the nucleus of our Association. My cousin, the late Rev. Bernard Shaw, Vicar of the Church of the Annunciation, Bryanston Street, was our Warden. To him and his sister, Miss Shaw, and to my commissary, Canon Bartlett, the Diocese of Nagpur in its infant days owes an immense debt of gratitude. Friends since departed, the Honourable Harriett Brodrick and Mrs. Huth, gave us large donations. For many years our Association sent us several hundred pounds every year, which enabled us to carry through schemes of great importance which would otherwise have been impossible. Those who, in regard for our great and venerable missionary societies, minimise the usefulness of Diocesan Associations, have never had to face the task of starting a new Diocese in foreign parts. Personal friendships and personal knowledge of the Bishop, of his work and workers, have an immense influence in attracting help often from unexpected quarters. Without our Nagpur Diocesan Association we should have fared very badly. During my time in England I had interviews with most of our great missionary societies, the C.M.S., S.P.G., S.P.C.K., and C.E.Z.M.S. Bishop Montgomery was kindness itself. His intimate knowledge of India made him fully realise some of the needs for which help was most urgently wanted. Through his influence the Society enabled us to start a chaplaincy at Bandikui and to receive help for our Bishop Cotton School,

Nagpur. I also met the Council of the Indian Church Aid Association, then presided over by Bishop Johnson, who promised me all the help in their power. I spent a pleasant day at Lambeth and found, as all overseas Bishops always found, a warm welcome and deep sympathy from the Archbishop and Mrs. Davidson. Nearly every Sunday I preached somewhere and usually got considerable financial help for my Diocese. On one memorable Sunday I preached in St. Paul's Cathedral in the morning, and in Canterbury Cathedral in the evening! I had the honour of receiving an invitation to the Lord Mayor's Banquet for Home and Overseas Bishops, and to the Secretary of State for India, Lord Morley's, dinner on the King's Birthday. At the latter I sat next to Sir Alfred Lyall and heard his views on the difficult problem of the Anglo-Indians.

Before returning to India I had more than one interview with our famous Church architect, Mr. G. F. Bodley, and his partner, Mr. Hare. It had been decided after long discussion and much consultation that All Saints' Church, Nagpur, was to be enlarged and become the Cathedral Church of the Diocese. We had been guided, I feel confident very wisely, to abandon the idea of building a new and expensive Cathedral. The Diocese had been formed to help the spiritual life of the widely scattered communities, most of them far remote from Nagpur. We needed all we could raise to build small Churches to strengthen our schools and to help our missions. Plans had been submitted for the enlargement of All Saints', Nagpur, by the Local Public Works Department, and by the architect for the Government of India, but as neither of them pleased us, I obtained permission to bring to England numerous full scale plans and large photographs of the Church prepared by the Public Works Department. These I handed over to Mr. Bodley. I can still see him in his office examining those plans most carefully, and can hear him saying, " We must make your Church one in which all who enter will feel drawn to pray." How his genius made the station Church of Nagpur into our beloved little Cathedral is well known to all who know Nagpur. I returned to India in the autumn of 1906 with renewed feelings of hope.

The year 1907 after my return from leave in England was, as usual, a very busy one with plenty of journeying in every part of the Diocese. Its special events were a fortnight's visit to the neighbouring Diocese of Chota Nagpur in the rainy season to hold confirmations for Bishop Foss Westcott, who was on sick leave in England, and a visitation of the Diocese by the Metropolitan of India in the cold weather. I shall allude later on to the remarkable and sad contrast between the enormous success of missionary work amongst the aborigines in Chota Nagpur, and the meagre results in the aboriginal missions in the Central Provinces and Rajputana.

About the visitation of a Diocese by the Metropolitan, a few words of explanation are needed for persons unversed in matters ecclesiastical. It is one of the duties of the Metropolitan of an ecclesiastical Province to hold periodical (once in five years) visitations or inspections of the Dioceses in the Province. This is done regularly in India. When the Metropolitan enters a Diocese officially on visitation, for the time being the Diocesan Bishop's powers are in abeyance. All the clergy of the Diocese and faithful laity may come to the Metropolitan and pour out their grievances to him. If they have some special complaint against their Bishop it will be heard! A famous London clergyman of a past generation once told his congregation that when he heard that the Bishop was about to hold a visitation of his clergy he looked up the dictionary and found that " a visitation was a dispensation of Providence sent to chastise us for our sins "! All I need say of Bishop Copleston's visitation was (as I wrote in my quarterly letter in December 1907), that everyone of us, especially the Bishop of the Diocese and his clergy, felt extremely sorry when it was over and he returned to Calcutta.

CHAPTER III

EARLY in 1908 I moved my headquarters to Nagpur, the capital of the Central Provinces. It was rather a wrench leaving Jubbulpore, a place I liked so much, but I had said in my first visitation charge in 1904 that I was quite prepared to sacrifice my personal inclinations if I was convinced that it was the best thing for the Diocese. As this had become increasingly clear to me I felt I must go. Looking back now across the years which have passed since then I thank the "Kindly Light" that guided me to Jubbulpore for those early years and then made it clear to me that I must "break up camp" and move on. The time was opportune. The unsympathetic and indifferent feelings which had been manifest at Nagpur amongst the leading officials when the scheme for a C.P. Bishopric was first mooted (largely determined, so I gathered, by fears of increased and unnecessary expense) had quite passed away. There was now a strong feeling in Nagpur that their Bishop should throw in his lot with them, and live amongst them. Jubbulpore, which had always been keen about the Bishopric, felt perhaps a little hurt that the Bishop was leaving his first love, but they, too, felt that no one would ever leave such an earthly Paradise as Jubbulpore to dwell in the heat of Nagpur unless a clear sense of duty called him. And the response which was soon manifest after my move, was made quickly, removing any feelings of regret I had experienced during the period of breaking up house.

For the next two years until Bishop's Lodge was built, I found a very pleasant home with Archdeacon the Venerable C. J. Palmer at Cathedral House. 1908 is a year full of inter-

esting memories.   It was the year of the Pan-Anglican
Congress, planned and organised so splendidly by Bishop
Montgomery.   This was followed by the Lambeth Conference
of Bishops, formerly spoken of as the Pan-Anglican Synod.
Every Diocese of the Anglican Communion was invited to
send a thank-offering to be presented in St. Paul's Cathedral
on the last day of the Congress.   Our infant Diocese sent a
substantial gift of £100, which was presented by Archdeacon
Davies, then on leave.   I took three months' leave to attend the
Lambeth Conference, and on my return wrote a very full
account of all I had seen and heard.   We published in our
Diocesan Quarterly for the next year or so very full statements
of the principal subjects discussed by the Bishops, and their
resolutions, so that the Diocese knew pretty well all its
important decisions.   One happy result for our Diocese was
that when a large sum of the Pan-Anglican thank-offering,
which was allocated to the needs of India, was being distributed by the Indian Bishops, I persuaded them to give a
substantial amount, nearly £3,000, to the Nagpur Diocese.
It proved an immense help in carrying out Mr. Bodley's extension of Nagpur Cathedral.   Later on we received from the
same source £1,500 for our English Church Schools.   I should
mention that while in England I developed still further the
Nagpur Diocesan Association with the help of my old friend,
Canon Bartlett.   In the latter part of 1908 Archdeacon Davies
finally decided to retire and Archdeacon Palmer took his place.

The winter of 1908 witnessed a very interesting event in
Nagpur, when an Industrial and Art Exhibition was held for
some weeks, which was attended by people from all over the
Central Provinces and other parts of India.   It had been
admirably planned and organised by Mr., afterwards Sir R.
Craddock, and was intended to stimulate and educate the
people.   It was at this Exhibition I first saw a cinema.   The
film was a journey through Switzerland, and I shall never
forget the remarks made by a group of Indian gentlemen at
the picture of a Swiss town with snow mountains in the
neighbourhood, which they mistook for Delhi!   The Nagpur
Exhibition, which was a great success and did a good deal to

educate the many who came to it, was marred by a painful incident, when some ill-advised Indian students, egged on doubtlessly by some revolutionaries, mutilated hopelessly the beautiful marble statue of Queen Victoria. After a considerable time the mutilated statue, which had been completely surrounded by some hoardings, was thrown into our principal reservoir, and a new statue, identical with the old one, was subscribed for by the loyal Indian residents of Nagpur. It now stands by the Legislative Building, our Central Provinces Parliament House. The Indian people had a great reverence for the great White Queen. When another of her statues was unveiled at Jubbulpore, some Indians placed cocoanuts and other offerings at the base. A zealous missionary who was present at the ceremony protested to the Chief Commissioner at this idolatry! I have no doubt that some of the uneducated of these Indians regarded the statue of this great lady as that of a goddess. Shortly after her death a student at the Morris College, Nagpur, concluded an essay on Queen Victoria with the words:

> "Dust to dust, and ashes to ashes,
> Into her tomb the great Queen dashes."

My winter touring in my own Diocese in 1908—9 was considerably broken into by a visit to Burmah on special duty. Dr. Arthur Mesac Knight, the Bishop of Rangoon, had been absent from his Diocese for some months suffering from an illness which unfortunately compelled him to resign. As there were a number of persons needing confirmation, Bishop Copleston arranged with the Indian Government that one of the Indian Bishops should go over to Burmah, and I was asked to undertake this interesting duty. It certainly remains amongst the very pleasant memories of my life. Everywhere I went in Burmah I learnt how deeply attached both clergy and laity were to their absent Bishop, and how greatly they longed for him to come back to them. Ten years before I had spent several months in China and Japan visiting different missions, so that the sight of these Mongolian people in Burmah with their bright and often merry faces, "the Irishmen of the East," so unlike the sadder faces of India, made me feel I was

D

back again in the Far East.   A fairly extensive confirmation tour had been arranged for me by Archdeacon Cory, which included Moulmein on the Salween river, the Karen Mission, Mandalay, Meiktila, Shwebo, and Maymyo, and lastly Rangoon itself.   The Karens are an aboriginal race in Burmah of Mongolian stock, and many of them have become Christians.   The Baptist missionaries have been specially successful. There was apparently a widespread belief that a person with red hair should bring them great blessings, so when Mrs. Mason, with a splendid head of red hair, appeared, they accepted her as the fulfilment of this prophecy, and many became Christians.

Through the great kindness of the Lt.-Governor of Burmah, Sir H. Thirkell White, I was able to go to Myitkina, then the most northern state in Upper Burmah, and to come down the Irrawaddy through the Defiles in a small Government steamer to Bhamo and Mandalay.   The great river between Myitkina and " the Defiles " is a sight one can never forget.   It is surrounded by vast forests with big mountain ranges on its left bank, the Chinese side, which separate the Irrawaddy from two other great rivers, the Salween, and the Mekong.   One has the feeling of being cut off from the world of men, and being alone with God and nature in the denseness of these forests.   What " the Defiles " of the Irrawaddy really mean will be better understood if we realise that when this gigantic river is in flood, it rushes through these " Defiles " 120 feet higher than when we passed through them in February.   My companion on this trip to Myitkina was the Rev. R. S. Fyffe, who succeeded Bishop Knight as Bishop of Rangoon a few months later.

On my return from Burmah I found Bishop's Lodge, which was to be the official residence of the Bishops of Nagpur, steadily rising from the ground.   I had been offered by Government a house to be built by the Public Works Department for which a rent would be charged, or a house built by myself from a Government loan of 4%, the interest to be paid annually and the total capital sum to be repaid in sixty years. Under the advice of one of the leading officials I accepted the

BISHOP'S LODGE, NAGPUR

latter suggestion. A fine design was given me by Sir Swinton Jacob of Rajputana fame, which after it had undergone certain modifications (largely to save expense) has been the residence of the Bishops of Nagpur since its completion early in 1910. I have always felt how much I and my successor owe to the Government for this kind arrangement, as Bishop's Lodge will ultimately become Church property and the annual interest and payment into a sinking Fund was so moderate as to be no drain on the Bishop's income.

In February 1910 I was married to Miss Lilian Agnes Haig at St. George's Church, Hoshangabad. To her I feel sure both I and my Diocese owe far more than I shall ever be able to tell. She entered into our life wholeheartedly, and endeared herself to everyone. She enjoyed our roughings, with their long and often fatiguing rides under an Indian sun, when visiting our scattered jungle Missions in the Gond, Bhil and Chanda Missions. One of our riding friends who rode in our paper chases used to say that she rode as if she had nine necks! I should add that the Central Provinces' Commission presented us with a very handsome solid silver tray beautifully inscribed, and that my clergy gave me the writing table which I still use. Some touching gifts came to us, too, from our Indian Christian friends.

Early in 1910 Archdeacon and Mrs. Charles Palmer left India on leave preparatory to retirement. He was succeeded by the Rev. Cyril Price as Archdeacon of Nagpur and senior Chaplain in charge of our Cathedral. He held the post for eight years and his work both in Nagpur and the Diocese was regarded by all of us, both clergy and laity, as of the highest value. I knew I could always rely on his advice. He was an excellent man of business, a very thoughtful preacher and endowed fully with sanctified common sense. I feel that I owe a special debt of gratitude for the help he gave me in those early days.

I held my second Visitation and third Conference in August 1910.

A little more than seven years had passed since I was enthroned in All Saints' Church, Nagpur. Then, as I have already stated, I was uncertain as to where my headquarters were to be. Now all uncertainty had happily passed away. I was living in Nagpur, in what we hope will be the permanent residence of the Bishops of the Diocese for the future. My Archdeacon was living in a suitable residence within the grounds of the Cathedral, and a smaller bungalow had been built not far away for the Assistant Chaplain. The work on the enlargement of our Cathedral, according to the plans of the late Mr. G. F. Bodley, had begun under the careful super-vision of Mr. G. M. Harriott, the head official of the Public Works Department, and would be continued so we hoped, if sufficient funds were available, for the next two or three years. But, best of all, the Scottish Episcopal Church had responded to my appeal, and had sent to live amongst us in Nagpur one of the Chanda Mission clergy, the Rev. G. D. Philip, and his wife. It is true that before this the Mission had supported Catechists, Schoolmasters, and even a Tamil clergyman to look after our Indian Christian people, mainly Mahrattas and Tamils. With the arrival of Mr. and Mrs. Philip, a much needed institution, an orphanage for poor Anglo-Indian children, was started and was looked after by them till we were in a position to make it a Diocesan Institution, under the care of a Diocesan Lady Worker.

Let me say a few words about this Orphanage. An official had told me of a number of very poor Anglo-Indian children who were being brought up in wretched homes without decent clothes, or food, or education. He promised me considerable help from his own pocket if I could do anything effective. But what could I do? We needed a suitable house in which to house them, a suitable person to act as matron or superin-tendent, funds to feed them and clothe them, and to pay for their education. Never has any good desire I have entertained been translated so soon into a delightful reality. I went to talk things over with Mr. and Mrs. Philip, who had only just arrived in Nagpur. They had a large mission bungalow, and within an hour or two these devoted people had decided to divide their bungalow into two parts and take in as many children as it would hold. Mrs. Philip was a fully trained

nurse. She had been a member of the Universities' Mission to
Central Africa, a warm friend of Bishop Frank Weston of
blessed memory. In no time about twenty of these little waifs
and strays were happily housed. Everyone in Nagpur and the
Diocese generously responded; funds were never lacking. Mrs.
Philip was always busy, especially when all the twenty
orphans went down at the same time with mumps and measles,
and she had to do all the nursing! Of such is the Kingdom
of Heaven! I shall tell later on how this beginning grew into
our All Saints' Children's Home with its handsome building
in the Cathedral grounds. The children received their education at the Bishop Cotton School in Nagpur.

My second visitation and the conference which followed
passed off most happily. I think we all felt that things were
beginning to move in the right direction. There is always an
element of sadness in such gatherings, for India is a land of
change, and as the Persian proverb puts it, " Earth's meetings
are always partings." We missed greatly some of the clergy
who had retired, and some who had passed on to the higher
life; but we were beginning to look forward and hoping that
with God's help we would make the new Diocese a living
reality.

In this, the second of the six charges I delivered to the clergy
during the twenty-three years I was their Bishop, I dwelt on
some of the needs which had become apparent to me during
the last seven years. I spoke of the importance of keeping
up our studies, especially our studies of Holy Scripture and
theology. I urged the formation of study circles, when
occasionally those clergy who lived not too far from larger
centres like Nagpur, Jubbulpore, Mhow and Ajmeer, might
meet for a day or two for brotherly fellowship and study.
The isolation of many of our chaplains and missionaries in
India is often very great and very trying! I dwelt on the
importance of visiting out-stations where little groups of
Europeans and Anglo-Indians in Government service or railway employ needed so much encouragement in their Christian
witness in a non-Christian atmosphere. I urged them to
approach suitable laymen in such out-stations with a view to

their gathering together on Sundays these isolated people for a Christian Service, when no ordained clergyman was available. I spoke, too, of the importance of our work amongst the British soldiers in our garrison stations; and later on in this and other conferences we discussed the various ways in which our chaplains could help them. Are there any young fellows who need our sympathy and help more than these soldier boys of ours in India? There they are, still quite young, exposed to many temptations, often feeling terribly lonely though surrounded by other fellows. They do respond marvellously to the parson they like. It is not enough for a Chaplain to preach to them from the pulpit at a parade service, though they do like a man who can really give them a rousing message of encouragement and hope. Their chaplain must let them see that he is their real friend, out to help them in every way. He must meet them in the Institute, join with them when he can in their games, and if his one great desire is to lead them to Christ he will have opportunities when he least expects them. I shall never forget the work that the late Bishop Bevan, then Bishop of Swansea, did especially for the Brecknock Regiment when he was with us in Mhow during the Great War. To him those " break-neck " boys, as they were amusingly called, nearly 800, were like his own children. After long night marches they would often find him with cauldrons of cocoa and tea at daybreak by some roadside waiting for his boys. He had prepared a large number of them for confirmation, and asked me before he returned to his Welsh Diocese to allow him to confirm them. Needless to say, I did so most gladly. Our Chaplain in Mhow became his very warm friend and used to describe the Bishop as his Episcopal Curate! At this visitation we had with us Father Holmes of the Oxford Mission, whose spiritual addresses at our celebration and intercession services were a great help and stimulus. He and his brothers of the Oxford Mission were always the truest friends of the Nagpur Diocese. During my twenty-three years' episcopate we often had visits from Father Brown, and I can recall very helpful visits from Studdert Kennedy of the Dublin University Mission, Canon Fisher of the S.P.G. Cawnpore Brotherhood, and Canon Rivington of the Bombay Diocese. Such wholehearted spiritual men are a tremendous boon to the Church of India. They have a message of life and power which they have received from the Source of all Life in their hours of communion with Him.

CHAPTER IV

THE CORONATION YEAR. 1911—12

On leave—Palestine—The Coronation—The Delhi Durbar—The King
and Queen visit Nagpur.

IN the Spring of 1911 I took eight months' leave out of India
for the purpose of a thorough rest.   My wife and I spent five
weeks in Palestine on the way home.   We left our P. & O.
steamer at Port Said, and boarded a Lloyd Triestino steamer
which took us up to Beyrout.   As she was carrying cargo and
spent twelve hours one day discharging it at Jaffa, and another
day at Haifa, we had two very interesting days on shore at
both these places.   Jaffa, with its orange groves, and Ramleh,
and Ludd, the ancient Lydda, are most interesting, and the
view from Mount Carmel above Haifa was really splendid.
From Beyrout we journeyed to Baalbec, where we spent a
whole day wandering amongst its wonderful ruined temples of
Jupiter, Venus and Bacchus, erected, so it is said, by a Roman
Emperor to counteract the influence of the Christian religion
which was spreading rapidly in Syria.   At Damascus, where
we spent several days, I visited the Syrian Patriarch, and he
did me the great honour of returning my visit.   All the staff of
our hotel were immensely excited and knelt on the stairs and
in the passages to receive his blessing.   His main conversation
was with my wife on the subject of the many ways in which a
wife could help her husband !   On my arrival at Beyrout I
had received a telegram from Bishop Blyth, then Bishop in
Jerusalem, asking me to take confirmation for him at Safed
and Nazareth.   I had wired back saying how gladly I would
do so, though where Safed was I had not the faintest idea !
However, I soon learnt when I got to Damascus that Safed
lies in the mountains above the Sea of Galilee at an elevation
of about 4,000 feet, and that it was a famous centre of
Rabbinic learning.   Our days on the Lake of Galilee were to
both of us days we can never forget.   While at Tiberias we

42

met a very gifted American lady artist who was engaged in painting a picture of the scene at the Lake when our Blessed Saviour restored St. Peter after the three times repeated question, " Simon, Son of John, lovest thou me? " We saw the artist's studies; I gave her the Communion early one morning at her special request. The picture is now hanging, so I understand, in the Chapel of the Central Jail of New York State, to give hope to men and women who have lost all hope in this world. Our visit to Safed, which is, I believe, " the City set on a hill which cannot be hid " was rather a surprise to us. Expecting it to be rather in the wilds and having to cross the Lake in a boat and to pick up our horses at the other side, I was clad in an old khaki coat and riding breeches, nor was my wife arrayed in anything much better. Judge our surprise when we rode into an extremely well-dressed little body of English missionaries. However, my Church robes removed the shock of our riding kit, and we had a delightful time with glorious views of Mount Hermon and Lake Merom. When returning to Tiberias the next morning, it was blowing a gale, and the Sea of Galilee was lashed into such a fury that no boat could venture on it. During the hour we spent riding along the shores of the Lake the wind had fallen and when we reached Tiberias it was " a great calm." Travelling behind us we learnt afterwards was the ill-fated heir to the Austrian Throne, Franz-Ferdinand and his wife. At Nazareth I held another confirmation, and from there we rode for two days accompanied by our Syrian dragoman named Andrew. On our first day we visited Nain, ate our sandwiches at Gideon's Pool, and rode on to Yenin, the southern side of the great plain of Esdraelon. Here we ran into a party of American tourists from Texas, men and women, whom we found most pleasant. They were wonderfully well mounted, and loved riding through the country, but what they knew of Palestine or wanted to know made me wonder why they had taken so much trouble to come there. The ride to Samaria and on to Nablus, ancient Shechem, was most interesting. While there we visited the Samaritan High Priest, and saw a copy of the Samaritan Pentateuch.

We also ascended Mount Ebal, the Mount of Blessing, and descended on the far side to the foot of the mountain to visit Jacob's well.

Everyone who visited Jerusalem in those days was sure of a warm welcome from the late Bishop Blyth. In his earlier days he had been Archdeacon of Rangoon. Our Church owes a great deal to Bishop Blyth for the wonderful way in which he established friendly relations between the Anglican and Greek Churches, and for the beautiful Cathedral of St. George which he was largely instrumental in building. The schools connected with the Cathedral, especially the Girls' School, were held in such esteem that, as I learnt when I was in Mesopotamia during the War, Baghdadi Christian girls were sent there across the desert for their education. Shortly before our arrival in Palestine, a serious dispute between the Turkish authorities and the Greek Church had been settled and the Greek Patriarch was back in Jerusalem. I got an introduction to him through Bishop Blyth, and after my visit was given a special place of honour when his Beatitude washed the feet of the Archimandrites on Maundy Thursday in the Court of the Church of the Holy Sepulchre. I had the privilege of assisting Bishop Blyth at his annual confirmation when I gave the addresses, and confirmed the men and boys. Visits to the Dead Sea, where I had a refreshing swim, and to Hebron where we saw the Mosque which encloses the Cave of Macpelah, brought our tour to a pleasant end. In a book by Baldensperger, a German writer, called " The Immutable East," the writer, who had lived for years in Palestine, shows how ideas and beliefs which go back to Old Testament days have survived through all the centuries of change which this small country has passed through. Especially this is true of dreams and visions, and the stories our dragoman told us of mothers having visions of patriarchs and prophets before the birth of their children, who requested them to name the unborn child after them, often in opposition to the relatives' wishes, were highly entertaining! If I have dwelt at undue length on our tour in Palestine it is because, for the next year or so after our return to India, I lectured

constantly about it in various parts of the Diocese, assisted
by really splendid slides which I had purchased in Jerusalem.

When we arrived in London at the end of April, 1911, the
approaching Coronation of King George and Queen Mary
was the thought uppermost in everybody's mind. Thanks to
the kindness of the India Office, I was provided with a seat in
the northern aisle of the Nave of Westminster Abbey, and,
though it was impossible from there to see the actual Coronation, still the brilliant scenes within the Abbey, the solemn
procession of the King and Queen to and from the chancel
where they were crowned, and the minor processions of the
foreign Princes with their brilliant uniforms, will ever remain
in one's memory. There certainly was a murmur of great
goodwill when the Crown Prince of Germany, who had so
recently visited India, proceeded to his appointed place. Unfortunately, during the period of our holiday, my wife's health
compelled her to keep absolutely quiet, so the only function
connected with the Coronation which she could attend was the
Thanksgiving Service in St. Paul's Cathedral, when our King
and Queen drove through the city to the great Cathedral to
give thanks to God for all His mercies vouchsafed to them and
to their people. On this occasion the Bishop of London, with
his usual kindness, gave us two of his seats in the choir.

It was during this holiday when I was addressing the
Representation Council of the Episcopal Church of Scotland
that I made an appeal for a lady worker to come out to
Nagpur, and work amongst the Anglo-Indian community. A
month or so later Miss Constance Ramsay, of Perth, who had
heard of this need, offered her services, which were gladly
accepted. She returned with us to India early in November,
and for the next sixteen years, with slight interruptions, when
she visited first Kenya, and then her people in Scotland, gave
herself wholeheartedly to the work as a purely voluntary
worker. Amongst her many good deeds was the starting of the
Girl Guides in Nagpur, which, beginning with a handful of
girls, is now a large and flourishing institution. During her
last visit to Scotland, one of our Anglo-Indian girls in the
Cathedral congregation wrote to her imploring her to return.

She said in her letter, " We feel as sheep without a shepherd,"
regardless of the fact of the presence in Nagpur of the Bishop,
the Archdeacon, a junior chaplain, a Scottish missionary priest
and two Indian priests! While I was at home I was, as usual
during leave in England, preaching and speaking a great deal
about India. My wife and I visited several of the Scottish
Bishops and spoke about their missionary work in Chanda
and Nagpur. I succeeded in finding two fresh chaplains for
our Additional Clergy Society and received some very
generous gifts towards our Cathedral. We arrived back in
Nagpur about the middle of November, and I was soon up to
the eyes in arranging work for the winter's touring.

December 1911 will always be remembered in India as the
month of the Coronation Durbar at Delhi. It was the first
time that a King and Queen of England had visited India,
and for this reason it was marked, as it should be, with
peculiar ceremonial grandeur. If I am able to describe the
impressions which the Delhi Durbar left on me twenty-three
years ago it is because the Editor of the Nagpur Diocesan
Magazine made me solemnly promise that, as I was one of the
fortunate ones who had been invited to Delhi, I would give
as vivid an impression as I could for the less fortunate ones
who would not be there. My first feeling when endeavouring
to fulfil my promise was, I know, that unless one was to write
a large book, copiously illustrated, it would be better to keep
silent. " For the Delhi Durbar was a triumph of organisa-
tion and brilliant scenes such as few living may hope to see
again." There was, however, so nearly everyone said, one
thing missing, and as it concerns the character of the Indian
Bishops it may be well to mention it. Why did not their
Imperial Majesties ride on a royal elephant in their state entry
into Delhi? When, as Prince and Princess of Wales, they had
entered Gwalior at Christmas 1905, they had ridden on a
magnificent elephant gorgeously decorated with the royal
umbrella over their heads! Why not, then, on this far greater
occasion? A day or two later the real reason for what seemed
to many a grave omission was given in a Mohammedan paper
at Delhi. " It would seem that in ancient days when Hindu

Emperors rode on their royal elephants, none but a Brahmin of the highest sanctity might drive the royal animal as he alone was worthy of sitting with his back to the King. And in Mohammedan days the most saintly Sayid had to be found for this important task, and though the Editor of this Mohammedan paper understood that there was no lack of saintliness among our Indian Bishops, he believed that none of them can sit like the saintly Brahmins and Sayids of olden days behind the ears of an elephant, and coax and cajole it along."

And so the obvious comment was that before the next Coronation Durbar the Government of India must request the Metropolitan of India to order one of his younger Bishops to qualify himself as a " Mahout " and so remove this scandal from the Church!

Every function was good at the Delhi Durbar, and each was better than the last. The Parade Service on Sunday, December 10th, was so well arranged that almost everyone could hear and see; and when one remembers that the congregation ran into several thousands, that is saying a good deal. An admirable sermon was preached by Bishop Whitehead, of Madras. It was, as General Count von Dohna of the Prussian Guards remarked to me, a very solemn service. Seven of our Indian Bishops were present, but owing to illness the Metropolitan of India, Bishop Reginald Copleston, was unfortunately absent.

Then came the presentation of colours to seven British, Scotch, and Irish Regiments, and afterwards to several Indian Regiments, which was one of the prettiest sights I have ever seen. What made it so striking a spectacle was the perfect lines which the several regiments kept and the sharp contrast in colour between the uniform of the Highland, Rifle, Redcoated, and Indian Regiments. But of course everything found its climax in the great Durbar itself, when the King Emperor and the Queen Empress in their royal robes faced on thrones on the smaller of two regal daises twelve thousand of the notabilities of their Indian Empire, Native Princes, Governors, Lieutenant-Governors, Chief Commissioners, and officials and their wives from all parts of India and Burmah. What could have been more interesting than to see these Indian

Princes making their obeisance; and Governors leading up
representative nobles and high officials to do homage? And
when this first portion of the ceremony was over, their
Majesties, leaving the thrones on the lower dais, crossed over
to thrones on the higher dais, and faced 50,000 of their Indian
subjects who were sitting or standing before them in a huge
crescent form. And what a crescent it was! In one portion
one could see nothing but blue turbans; in another, yellow;
in another, saffron; in another, white. The artistic grouping
on so large a scale was magnificent. And then came the great
announcement that Delhi was to be the capital of India, and
Calcutta, founded more than 200 years previously by Job
Charnock on the banks of the Hoogley, was to be like Bombay
and Madras, merely a provincial capital!

Next to the Durbar came the Investiture when the
Sovereign himself, as the fountain of honour, dispenses those
rewards which he has created. It was an evening function
held in a vast Shamiana or Pavilion Tent capable of holding
two or three thousand people. The spectacle was a very
brilliant one; Indian Princes, military officers in their scarlet
uniforms, civil and political officers in their levee dress, half a
dozen Bishops in red convocation robes, and a great multitude
of fair ladies with dresses fresh from Paris and London. And
while the solemn investiture was proceeding in its usual digni-
fied manner, and every eye was fixed on the King as he laid
the royal sword on the shoulders of many whom we knew,
there arose loud shouts of fire, and the shrill noise of fire
whistles outside the Shamiana! For a moment or two everyone rose from their seats, but a few commanding shouts of
" sit down " allayed any panic; and all the time the King
continued his task with perfect composure. Few realised till
afterwards how near we had been to what might have been
an appalling tragedy, for within forty yards of the Shamiana
a smaller tent had caught fire from an overturned lamp, and
had it been a windy night this investiture would have ended in
grim tragedy.

Few even of those accustomed to a military review at
Aldershot will ever forget the greatest review which India

has ever witnessed some miles away from Delhi. From every part of India our soldiers, British and Indian, had been brought to take part in it. There were there great masses of men moving in perfect order, the long, straight lines of our Cavalry Regiments in full gallop, and the mad rush of the Horse Gunners sweeping past their Majesties. And then came the time when this great city of white canvas, so beautifully laid out in its various camps (we were living in the Central Provinces Camp as guests of the Chief Commissioner), began to melt away and those who had been feasting in Olympus for a whole fortnight returned to the ordinary duties of life.

But for us in Nagpur all was not yet over, for only a few weeks later our King and Queen were driving through our streets responding graciously to the loyal greetings of thousands of their Indian subjects. It was a most gracious act on their part when journeying from Calcutta to Bombay to halt for a short period at the capital of the Central Provinces, and from the Fort of Sitabaldi to view our large Mahratta city. A suitable monument marks the spot where they stood, and Nagpur, like London, has its Kingsway along which they drove on this memorable occasion. It is well to remember that within twenty-four hours of their arrival in London, the King and Queen, accompanied by other members of the Royal family, were in St. Paul's Cathedral taking part in a public act of thanksgiving for the safe and happy completion of their great enterprise.

"Through three months of a dark winter," said the Archbishop of Canterbury, "we at home have daily prayed that God would preserve, by land and sea, our King and Queen, and that their journey might tend to increase goodwill among the people of India. Shall we fail now to give thanks for the rich, the almost startlingly rich answer to our prayer?"

CHAPTER V

A MEMORABLE YEAR. 1912

The Consecration of the Bishop of Dornakal in Calcutta—An epoch-making Synod and Conference.

THE year 1912 was a memorable one for our Church in India. The removal of the capital of India from Calcutta to Delhi had suggested to some the idea of the removal of the Primacy from Calcutta to a see of Delhi. There had been a growing feeling also, especially amongst a number of the clergy, that the various problems of the Church should not be left entirely in the hands of the Episcopal Synod, which met in private, and then published its resolutions and decisions. They asked for a wider and more representative body which should include both clergy and laity. It can be stated at once that they found no sort of opposition to this view amongst the Bishops, and when the Episcopal Synod met in Calcutta in February 1912, it was decided to hold another Synod in December 1912, and to summon clerical and lay delegates from all the Indian Dioceses to attend as assessors. To prepare these clerical and lay assessors for what would then come up for serious consideration as to the best method of synodical government in the Province, a very full memorandum was drawn up stating various points of view which had been brought before the Synod which they considered worthy of consideration. These points of view may be stated briefly. There were those who held that the Ecclesiastical Province of India, Burmah and Ceylon should be divided into two Ecclesiastical Provinces. They argued that if England needed two Ecclesiastical Provinces, Canterbury and York, a huge country like India must certainly need more than one Province and one Metropolitan. There were some who even suggested the removal of the Primacy from Calcutta to Delhi, having three Provinces with an Archbishop of Delhi. The pros and cons for these views were stated very fully in this memorandum, so that when the

50

assessors met the Bishops in a historic conference at Calcutta in December 1912, everybody who attended was more or less prepared for the discussions and the decisions which would be eventually taken.

Before the conference actually met an event of the first importance to the Church of India took place in the Cathedral of St. Paul, Calcutta, when Bishop Copleston, our Metropolitan, assisted by no less than ten of the Bishops of the Province, consecrated the Rev. Vedayanagam Samuel Azariah as Bishop of Dornakal in the Telugu country within the territories of the Nizam of Hyderabad. Years ago in 1900 when, as Head of the Dublin University Mission to Chota Nagpur, I was one of the speakers at the Annual Meeting of the S.P.G., Lord Hugh Cecil had spoken somewhat reproachfully of the fact that after so many years of work in India our Church had not consecrated any Indians to the Episcopate. I remember how Prebendary Tucker had asked me while on the platform to refer to this remark of his, and how Father Benson of the Cowley Fathers, the other speaker, had spoken of certain difficulties arising out of class and family jealousies in South India, which still lingered on as a heritage from old caste ideas. This reproach was now wiped away. The ceremony was most impressive; Dr. John Mott, the distinguished American Evangelist, who was present, said it was one of the most striking sights he had ever witnessed. The consecrating Bishops were all robed in their scarlet chimeres and the sermon was preached by Canon Sell of the Church Missionary Society, one of the veteran missionaries of our Church in India. Previous to the consecration various deputations of Indians, Christians from South India, had waited on the Bishop-Designate to present to him addresses of congratulation, and various gifts which included his Episcopal robes, an Episcopal ring, a pastoral staff, a pectoral cross, etc. It was abundantly evident that the consecration of our first Indian Bishop had roused lively interest and enthusiasm among a large section of the Indian Church. With his consecration the number of our Bishops in the Indian Province amounted to the Apostolic number of twelve. One recalled the fact how ninety-eight

E

years before our first Bishop East of Suez was consecrated for Calcutta, and now our Church in India, Burmah and Ceylon needed twelve Bishops to shepherd our growing flocks. Of those who took part in that ceremony none can have felt more joy than Bishop Whitehead of Madras. It was he who had discovered Bishop Azariah, a man who has been used so wonderfully by God in winning large numbers of his fellow countrymen to allegiance to the Lord Christ, and membership in His Church. It was he who was entrusting to him an important sphere of his own Diocese.

During the week following the consecration the Bishops sat in Synod. For the first three days they were assisted in their deliberations by forty-eight assessors, clerical and lay representatives of our various Indian Dioceses. The subjects discussed during those days were connected with the formation of a Synodical system of Church government throughout our Church in India. These discussions were full of interest and by no means devoid of humour. One Indian delegate delighted us all by telling the assembly that he had never dreamt we were such a nice lot of people! Before the delegates departed, many of them on journeys of considerably more than a thousand miles to Burmah, Ceylon, Tinnevelly and the Punjab, it was unanimously decided that each Diocese was to form a representative Synod or Council which was to deal with the Church affairs of its Diocese, and that these Diocesan Synods were to elect from these members, clerical and lay, representatives to sit on one central and provincial assembly (or Synod) to deal with the affairs of the Church as a whole. It was, however, made quite plain that, according to Catholic usage and tradition, the delicate questions of Church doctrine should be left with the Synod of Bishops, who might, however, summon specially trained men to sit with them as advisers and assessors, but without voting power. It was at this time that the question of the name of our Church in India was first raised. Nearly everyone was opposed to the title of the Church of England in India. One distinguished Indian, now alas departed, Dr. Rudra, Principal of St. Stephen's College, connected with the Cambridge Mission at Delhi, pleaded for the title, the Church of India : " Give us a Church with the name of our own country and we shall live for it and die for it." The title which at that time found most favour with both missionary and Indian delegates was " The Church of India in communion with the Church of England."

So ended this epoch-making gathering, which was to find its climax and consummation eighteen years later when through the passing of the Indian Church Act in Parliament in 1927, our Church in India, in March 1930, became an independent branch of the Anglican Communion with its own Canons and Constitution under the title of the Church of India, Burmah and Ceylon. For the next year or so every Diocese was busily engaged in Synod making. We were, I have always believed, exceptionally fortunate in the Nagpur Diocese, in having several of our senior clergy to whom consti-tution making was a fascinating pursuit ! The Rev. Canon Alex Wood, now Bishop of Nagpur, who had been brought up in the Episcopal Church of Scotland, had a peculiar flair for this task, and he was ably backed by my officiating Arch-deacon, F. W. Martin, Canon C. W. Darling, and the late Canon E. A. Hensley. The scheme for a provincial council or synod was entrusted to Bishop Lefroy, Bishop Whitehead and Bishop Palmer. I was entrusted with the task of collect-ing and tabulating the general principles of the provincial synods of other branches of the Anglican Communion. Shortly after our return to Nagpur from the Synod, Bishop and Mrs. Copleston paid us a farewell visit on their journey from Calcutta to Bombay. Deeply did we all grieve at his resigna-tion. He had been in the East for nearly forty years, first as Bishop of Colombo, and then as Bishop of Calcutta and Metropolitan of India. My wife and I have always remem-bered with pleasure the fact that the last house in India in which he and Mrs. Copleston stayed was Bishop's Lodge, Nagpur.

CHAPTER VI

OUR GREAT DAY. 1914

The consecration of All Saints' Cathedral, Nagpur—My third visitation—
A visit from the Metropolitan—My fourth visitation.

FEBRUARY 18th, 1914, was a great day in the history of the
Diocese of Nagpur. On the morning of this day, we reached
the goal for which we had been praying and working and
waiting for nine long years, when I consecrated nearly all of
what Mr. G. F. Bodley had designed to make the old station
Church of Nagpur into the Cathedral of the Diocese. Everyone who saw what his genius had created under conditions
which must have handicapped him greatly were loud in his
praises. We had a large congregation, some of them non-
Christians, to witness the ceremony of consecration. The
petition for consecration was read by Mr. J. K. (afterwards
Sir John) Batten, I.C.S., officiating judicial Commissioner.
The sermon was preached by the Venerable Cyril Price, Archdeacon of Nagpur. As it expressed so deeply the feelings of
many who were then present, I am venturing to quote several
of its most striking passages. Taking as his text,
Psalm xc. 16, "Show thy servants thy work and their
children thy glory," he stated, "This is a great day
for all of us, not only for us who are present but for
those in other parts of the world who have taken their
share in raising this building to the honour and glory
of Almighty God. Since the consecration of our Bishop
on Lady Day, 1903, there has been no day of equal importance in the history of the Diocese. We have come from all
parts of this widespread Diocese, some of us from places almost
a thousand miles away, to pray God to accept this one offering, this visible symbol of the fact that He does indeed dwell
amongst men, and of our belief in Christ Jesus our Lord.
This day we see the consummation of years of labour.
Though the Diocese is of vast extent, almost one-fifth of India,

54

ALL SAINTS' CATHEDRAL, NAGPUR

it is still small in point of number and very scattered. From Ajmeer and from the Bhils in far distant Rajputana, from the land of the Gonds to the north of us, and from Jubbulpore, from southern Gondland with its headquarters at Chanda, from every chaplaincy in the Diocese, and from our friends at home, help has come, from rich and poor, to build this Cathedral Church which we see to-day. It is nine years since the first efforts to raise the money were made, and just four years since the actual work began. It is not finished even now; much of the original plans and more in the way of beautifying and enriching it are left to future generations. The building which was consecrated to-day was designed by the greatest and most reverent architect of his day. It expresses our English conception of worship, of the dignity, the loftiness, the majesty of God and of how ' God in man draws near to man in God.' "

Later on in the morning when giving my third visitation charge to the clergy of the Diocese assembled in the Cathedral, I dwelt for a few moments on this same subject. I said, " When I look back to the time, nearly nine years ago, when the few who were interested in the scheme of its enlargement made their final decision as to what should be attempted; when I recall the difficulties of various kinds which stood in the way of doing anything really good in the improvement of the old Church, and when, with the memory of these difficulties still fairly fresh, I see the building in which we are worshipping this morning, I feel that we can indeed thank God for His goodness and take fresh courage for our future work." I cannot doubt but that it was through His guidance we were led to the choice of our architect, the late Mr. G. F. Bodley, whose genius as a Church architect was second to none in his generation. There is another reason why as a Church we may feel thankful at the accomplishment of our task. The money which has been spent on it has been almost entirely the gift of our own fellow churchmen in India and at home. With the exception of a comparatively small grant from Government of £500, based on the number of official sittings, the money has come from the Church itself. It is the Church's gift to

Him Whose worship and service we long to see recognised and loved by all in this land."

I also thanked most heartily the clergy of the Diocese for the splendid way they had backed me up all along in raising the large sum of money needed for the Cathedral. Some things come back very clearly to my memory in connection with our Cathedral. It was during the visit of our King and Queen to India as Prince and Princess of Wales in the winter of 1905—6, at the Christmas services at Gwalior, that we had our first Church collection for this object. Mr. Bodley had said to me during one of our interviews, " If you make the Church really devotional you will find numbers of people coming forward with gifts to beautify it." It was not long before we were to see how true was this remark. Two beautiful altars of marble, one the High Altar and the other in the Lady Chapel, were amongst our earliest gifts. They were made of beautiful Rajputana marble under the eye of Sir Swinton Jacob, from designs obtained in England. The east window by Burleson and Grylls was given by my wife and myself in memory of our fathers. A beautiful marble font was the gift of my former Chaplain, the Rev. G. E. M. Tonge. The Viceroy and Lady Hardinge, who had visited the Cathedral before it was completed, had given us a most generous gift which enabled us to carry out in fine Burmah teak wood the sedilia for our three canons. Money was generously subscribed for a three-manual Willis organ, towards which one member of the congregation, a young engineer, devoted to Church music and himself an organist, gave £500. Then with the conclusion of the War many beautiful gifts, most of them memorials of dear ones, who had either fallen or been miraculously preserved, were almost showered on us. In most cases the designs for such gifts were made or approved of by our architect, Mr. Hare. Beautiful crosses, vases and candlesticks were given for both altars, as well as handsome brass rails before the High Altar. A very fine bronze canopy for the marble font was presented by the late Sir Henry Drake Brockman, Judicial Commissioner of the Central Provinces, and Lady Drake Brockman, as a thankoffering. Three additional stained glass windows were also presented, one of them by the members of the Indian Civil Service in memory of one of their distinguished members who was drowned when the P. & O. SS. *Persia* was torpedoed off Crete; the second in memory of my eldest nephew, Adjutant of the 9th Gurkhas, who fell in Mesopotamia. The third stained glass window, a very beautiful piece of work of Powell's, was the War Memorial of the Central Provinces for British officers and men who fell in the War. I shall refer to this more fully later on.

One fact about All Saints' Cathedral deserves mention. When the smaller portion of it was originally built in 1863 as the station Church of Nagpur, it was built by private subscription, largely assisted by a Government grant. It was also put on the list of buildings to be maintained and repaired by Government. While it was greatly enlarged in accordance with Mr. Bodley's design with the full approval of Government, and while the Government merely contributed a small amount towards its enlargement, the responsibility of keeping it in repair was retained, which is certainly an enormous boon to a poor Diocese!

Little did we dream on that bright and happy day in February 1914 that within less than six months we should for four long years be offering within our Cathedral walls constant intercessions for our Empire and its peoples plunged in recurring sorrows and anxieties owing to the greatest war the world has ever seen. Perhaps it was only natural, but later on it seemed clearly providential, that on the day of the consecration of our Diocese's chief House of Prayer, the main burden of my visitation charge to the clergy should have been on the subject of prayer and especially of the power of Intercessory Prayer. No one has ever written more beautifully and convincingly on the subject of prayer than has that saintly man, William Law. It was his Serious Call to a holy life which was one of the most powerful influences in John Wesley's life. I read long passages from his description of Ouranious, the holy priest, who was never weary of bringing before God the needs and sins and sorrows of all he knew in intercessory prayer. Long years after, when I was bidding my Diocese a last farewell in April 1926, amongst several illuminated addresses which were presented to me and my wife, was one from our Cathedral congregation at Nagpur. It was carried out by an Indian artist with a charming miniature picture of the Cathedral at the top and a miniature picture of our Cathedral Hall which we used for Diocesan Councils and parochial purposes at the bottom. If I quote portions of its too kind and generous remarks, I do so mainly because it shows what our Cathedral at Nagpur has meant to so many of our devoted people in that place. " It is now many years, my Lord Bishop, since subsequent to your consecration in 1903 as the first Bishop of Nagpur, you took up your residence here, and associated yourself with the conduct of the various services in All Saints' Church. The landmarks you are leaving behind you testify to your constant pastoral care and consideration. All Saints' Church has been enlarged according to the design of a celebrated English architect into a fine Cathedral without losing the architectural features characterising the Church from the time of the formation of the Central Provinces. This Hall in which we have met this evening the congregation owes mainly to your generosity; and though it was built as a Cathedral Hall, it will always be known among us by your name, as the Chatterton Hall. Within this Cathedral enclosure stands the All Saints' Orphanage, brought into existence by you. The Cathedral organ and the beautiful War Memorial Window are adornments of the Church due to your fostering care. All these are the outward and visible signs of benefits bestowed, and will remain in perpetuity the heritage of All Saints' congregation, permanent memorials of your beneficent activity, and of the loving thought for those of your congregation who laid down their lives in the Great War. Above all, to those who have been members of the congregation during this period, the poignant memory will remain of the services of prayer and intercession, and then of praise and thanksgiving held by you during the World War. In particular, the memory of the services of continuous congregational prayer during the hard struggle of 1917, culminating in the services of thanksgiving and praise for the crowning mercies of victory and peace in 1918, will always be treasured, as well as the anniversary services since then held by you in your Cathedral Church which we have had the happiness to attend."

With the completion of our Cathedral the time was ripe for appointing, in accordance with ancient custom, certain of the clergy of the Diocese as Canons. As the total number of clergy in the Diocese at the time was only forty-seven, I felt it would be ridiculous to appoint more than three in addition to the Archdeacon. Two of the four selected were missionaries, the Rev. Canon Alex Wood, Head of the Scottish Episcopal Mission at Chanda, who has succeeded me as Bishop of Nagpur, and the late Rev. Canon E. A. Hensley, Secretary of the Church Missionary Society at Jubbulpore. The other Canon selected was the Rev. Charles W. Darling, Senior Government Chaplain, who, with my Archdeacon, the Venerable Cyril Price, represented the work for our English and Anglo-Indian people. The installation was duly carried out with full ceremony in the presence of nearly all the clergy of the Diocese at Choral Evensong, the Deed Poll creating the canonries being read by Mr. George Paris Dick, barrister at law and Government Advocate in the Central Provinces. Our Cathedral Constitution was a very simple one. We had examined carefully the constitution of other Cathedrals, especially those in India, and had discussed matters very carefully with all concerned. We had no need under the conditions of our work for the luxury of Deans, and needless to say all our Canons were honorary. The Bishop was the Dean of his Cathedral, and had the use of it for any Episcopal acts, and for Diocesan services and functions, provided that the regular services were not interrupted save with the concurrence of the Chaplain in charge of the Cathedral and parish. The Chaplain in charge was and is almost invariably.the Archdeacon of the Diocese, who is in charge of the parish, and is generally assisted by a junior Chaplain. At this time the Cathedral was actually the Parish Church of Nagpur, its Lady Chapel being generally used for the Indian services. Later on the handsome mission Church of St. Thomas was built largely by the efforts of the late Canon G. D. Philip of the Scottish Episcopal Mission. It was consecrated in 1925 in the presence of the Most Reverend Dr. Robberds, Primus of the Scottish Episcopal Church.

My third visitation was followed immediately by a Diocesan Conference. The main business of this Conference, which was attended by a large number of the leading laity of the Diocese, English and Indian, as well as by all the clergy, was to consider the Draft Constitution of a Diocesan Synod which had been prepared by a Committee appointed some months before. As I have already stated, the Synod of Bishops when assembled in Calcutta in December 1912 with fifty assessors, representative of all our Indian Dioceses, had unanimously decided that the time had come when synods ought to be established in every Diocese, and we were then gathered in conference to consider our Committee's Draft Constitution. One of the happiest episodes in the conference was a visit from Bishop G. A. Lefroy, who had succeeded Bishop Copleston as Bishop of Calcutta and Metropolitan of India. He spent a whole day with us and attended two of our conference sessions. On the evening of his arrival he addressed a largely attended meeting in the Museum Hall, when after having received an address of welcome from the Indian Christian Association, and having been duly garlanded, he delivered a very fine address on the meaning and value of synodical government. Our Committee was greatly encouraged in their work on our Draft Constitution by the Metropolitan's approval. He considered that they had made the best possible use of the draft which he and the Bishops of Madras and Bombay had drawn up at Bangalore, being neither too doctrinaire nor too sketchy. He informed us that he was shortly going on leave to England for a few months and would, while there, discuss with the Secretary of State for India and other high legal authorities, whether it would be possible while preserving our connection with the State to receive from it the freedom necessary to work our synods in a really effective manner. He spoke very clearly about what is involved in a "consensual compact" by which members of the Synod will bind themselves to obey its rulings, as synods were, he stated, legislative bodies and not merely debating societies! He finished his speech by saying that until the consensual compact is actually accepted the word Council rather than Synod should be used, though the machinery and some of the central features of a Synod could be introduced at once as a preparation for the time of complete freedom, whenever it is attained. This was the only occasion during the comparatively short period of his Metropolitanate that Bishop Lefroy visited Nagpur. He was with some other of our Bishops in Jubbulpore in the winter of 1916, and after that his health steadily declined owing to an aggravated form of arthritis which made active exercise most difficult. No one ever fought more bravely against pain and weakness. His love of India and his supreme desire to make Christ known in India kept him out there when it might have been wiser for him to retire. Happily for him, he never had to retire, for on the day he resigned he passed into the Presence of his Master. All that was mortal of him rests most suitably outside the eastern end of Calcutta Cathedral. Most certainly our present Metropolitan, Bishop Foss Westcott, and Bishop Palmer of Bombay, in the difficult and controversial days which they had to face before the passing of the Indian Church Act which in 1930 made our Church of India an independent branch of the Anglican Communion, must have always known how fully their old leader was with them in spirit. One other person who helped us greatly in this conference was Canon Cecil Stansfeld Rivington, of the Bombay Diocese. He had come specially at my invitation to give us his counsel, as his experience in the drafting of the constitution of the Bombay Synod would, I knew, be of especial value. He added still further to our indebtedness to him by the two beautiful addresses at our Holy Communion services on Thursday and Friday morning. The last time I had the privilege of meeting Canon Rivington was when I saw him in his Indian home at Betgiri Gadag, where for long years, living almost entirely among Indians, he prepared young Indian students for the Ministry of the Church. Like the famous German missionary, Schwartz, and Father Brown of the Oxford Mission, he spent over half a century in missionary work in India. He had come to India in 1878, and when he passed to his rest in 1933 he had given India fifty-five years of service without once visiting his native land !

At the final session of our Conference the following resolution was moved by the late Sir Henry Stanyon, and seconded by the Rev. Norman Marshall:

" This Conference is of opinion that Synodical government in this Diocese be established as completely and as early as possible; the Synod being composed of the Bishop, the clergy and lay representatives, and founded upon voluntary religious associations evidenced by a formal consensual compact."

1917

Three years later, in February 1917, shortly before my second visit to the troops in Mesopotamia, I held my fourth visitation followed by a Diocesan Conference. I did so because the Metropolitan, Bishop Lefroy, being uncertain when the War would be over, wished all the Dioceses of the Province to frame, without delay, the constitution of their Diocesan Councils. His conversations with the Secretary of State for India and distinguished ecclesiastical lawyers in England had made it clear that without a severance of State relations the Church in India could not possibly have fully constituted Synods with legislative authority, and so, for the word Synod, the word Council was everywhere used. It was during this Conference, held in those troublous times, that our Nagpur Diocesan Council was finally launched with its Standing Committee, and Boards of pastoral work, of education, and of missions. For eleven years since 1906 we had carried on the work of the Diocese with the simple machinery of the Diocesan Board. Now we were moving forward into a fuller development. To our Standing Committee was entrusted the important task of caring for the finances of the Diocese, and starting a system of assessing our various constituencies. My fourth visitation Charge was naturally coloured by thoughts of the

War, many of them suggested by my experiences in France and Mesopotamia. If in 1914 I had urged on my brother clergy the vital importance of intercessory prayer, and the getting into touch with individual souls by regular visiting, on this occasion I dwelt on the equally vital importance of having a living message from God of life and hope to men and women face to face with death. When I had my first experience of the War, for a short time in 1915 with the Indian Corps in France, speaking daily to men who might at any moment be face to face with their Creator, or suffering cruel agonies, I realised as never before the help a sermon might give if it was a real message from God with God's power behind it.

> " Word of mercy giving
> Succour to the living,
> Word of life supplying
> Comfort to the dying."

I used to find those words of the Child Saviour's, " I must be about my Father's business," a splendid opening in my talk to the men. Certainly if the War ought to have taught us clergy anything it was the hypocrisy of opening one's mouth to speak to men and women without a real conviction of the truth of our message.

CHAPTER VII

THE MISSIONARY WORK OF THE DIOCESE. OUR MISSIONARY WORK AMONGST ABORIGINES

(1) *The Gond Mission of the Church Missionary Society*

Started by Mr. Donald McLeod—Its first German missionaries at Karangia—A forgotten tragedy—Its earlier English missionaries and pioneer work—The Rev. Herbert Molony and band of evangelists at Marpha—Later missionaries—Tiger Price—Famine in Mandla District—Rev. Failbus' Gondi Grammar—Rev. Joshua Khalko—Agricultural Settlement—A Gond mystery man—Gond Mela—Sadhu Sunder Singh—Mission at Patpara—My tours in Gond-land.

A GOOD many people have rather vague ideas as to what an Indian Bishop's work actually is. I have been seriously asked sometimes by people who are interested in missions as to whether I had anything to do with them! They obviously thought that my real work was amongst British soldiers, civilians, and Anglo-Indians. As it was the call of the mission field which first took me to India, where I went at the end of 1891 as Head of the Dublin University Mission to Chota Nagpur, and as a great deal of my episcopal work was connected with our missionary efforts, I should like to give my readers some idea of what our missions are doing. We are not alone in our missionary enterprise in this huge field. My readers will be surprised and perhaps pained when I tell them that the number of our Anglican Missionaries—men and women—in this diocese is considerably less than one in ten of all the other Christian Missionaries. There is some truth in what the late Bishop Jacob of St. Albans said, that the American Free Churches are doing more than the Anglican Church for the conversion of India. There are Roman Catholic missions with a Bishop at Nagpur, and a Vicar-General at Ajmeer. There is a fine network of Scottish Presbyterian missions in Rajputana, long established and particularly strong in medical and educational work. The Canadian Presbyterian Church has some excellent missions in

Central India with an Indian Christian College at Indore. The Scottish Presbyterian Church has a very strong mission at Nagpur with a Christian College named after their famous missionary, Stephen Hyslop. There are strong American missions in the Central Provinces at Jubbulpore and elsewhere, the two most prominent being the Methodist Episcopal and the Disciples of Christ, a Baptist Church of which we know little in England. Our Anglican Church has six spheres of work, rather widely separated and not strongly staffed. Some years ago our staff of European missionaries, men and women, did not number forty—and to-day they are hardly fifty. The united staffs of the other bodies are well over 560.

The oldest of our Missions is carried on by the Church Missionary Society at Jubbulpore, in the northern part of the Central Provinces. From there it has developed its work amongst the Gonds in the Mandla District of the Satpura country. Away in the south of the Central Provinces the Scottish Episcopal Church has an interesting Mission with its headquarters at Chanda, the former capital of the southern Gond kingdom. In 1910, at my urgent request, this Mission opened a branch Mission at Nagpur. For the first twelve years of my episcopate, from 1903 to 1915, a very interesting mission amongst the Bhils in western India was in the Nagpur Diocese. When, however, it began to develop more into the Bombay Presidency and away from Rajputana, and when the Church in India adopted the system of representative Church Councils, it was felt wiser to hand it over to the Bombay Diocese. The wisdom and necessity for this will be more apparent when we realise that this Mission was about 300 miles from Bombay and nearly 1,000 miles from Nagpur! Our two other Missions in Rajputana, at Ajmeer and in the native state of Bharatpur, are supported by the S.P.G. and C.M.S. respectively. They are quite small and in both cases have an Indian clergyman in charge of the congregation. Let me endeavour to give some idea of the work of these Missions.

Our work at Jubbulpore and among the Gonds has an interesting history which goes back nearly 100 years. In 1831 Mr. Donald McLeod, an Indian civilian and brother-in-law of the late Bishop Montgomery, was sent by the Department of Government for the suppression of the Thugs, to work under Colonel Sir W. Sleeman, and was stationed at Saugor.   Later on he became Deputy Commissioner of Seoni, where he remained for several years.   He began to take a deep interest in this beautiful Satpura District and the simple-minded Gonds. He even wished to spend the remainder of his career among the Gonds, declining several better appointments in other parts of India.   He writes from Seoni, " I look upon my lot as fixed in this country, a land of wonderful interest, albeit at present in the darkness of night."   A few years later, in 1840, Mr. McLeod was appointed to Jubbulpore as Deputy Commissioner.   It was then that he carried out his long-conceived plan of commencing a Christian Mission among the Gonds. " He had long felt," so his biographer tells us, " that the simple habits of this primitive race afforded an admirable field for Christian effort, and he had for some time past endeavoured to enlist the sympathy and co-operation of Christian people at Calcutta and elsewhere in his cherished project.   He had written a long and interesting article on this subject in the ' Calcutta Christian Observer,' in which he endeavoured to show that the best plan was to start an agricultural mission settlement among them."   As no English missionary society was willing to take up this idea he acted upon it himself, and applied to Pastor Gossner of Berlin, who sent out to him a little band of German artisans and husbandmen (a carpenter, a schoolmaster, and an apothecary were amongst the number), to work amongst the Gonds.   They were placed under the superintendence of the Rev. Alois Loesch, a Lutheran minister, who had previously worked in South India.

The missionary band arrived at Jubbulpore in 1841 and shortly afterwards proceeded to the Satpura highlands, making their central station at the village of Karanjia, in the Mandla district, about fourteen miles from the source of the Nerbudda at Amarkantak.   There they lived in a simple fashion, building their bungalow with their own hands.   Shortly after their arrival at Karanjia, Mr. McLeod was able to pay them a visit. He was delighted at what appeared to be the happy commencement of favourable mission work amongst the Gonds. We have a few interesting lines from the pen of the leader of this missionary enterprise, the Rev. A. Loesch, which were written at this period, " Karanjia is one of the finest places I have ever seen in India; it is sixteen miles to the west of Amarkantak, and situated on the road to that place; it is often visited by hosts of fakirs and ghosains who extort the last coin from the poor ignorant Gonds, whom we shall no longer suffer to be maltreated by that idle and wicked set of people. The climate is almost European, the soil very fertile and water delicious."

The first few months had passed, and the sky seemed unclouded, when there fell on this small missionary band a calamity as sudden as it was terrible. Early in the rains an epidemic of cholera swept over this neighbourhood, and within a few weeks four of the mission band were dead, and a fifth lay between life and death. The doctor was unfortunately the first to die, and this fact may have been partly responsible for the death of the others. One of the survivors lost his reason, and died not long afterwards, the other joined Stephen Hyslop in Nagpur, and died three years later. Within a few months of its starting, the mission had ceased to exist. Such was the hard fate which befell Mr. McLeod's endeavours to establish a mission amongst the Gonds. That it should have ended with such tragic suddenness is all the more pathetic and mysterious when one is reminded of the fact that a somewhat similar mission sent about the same time by Pastor Gossner of Berlin to the aborigines of Chota Nagpur, led eventually to the conversion of tens of thousands of the Kols.

After Mr. McLeod's departure from Gondwana (he ultimately became Sir Donald McLeod, Lieutenant-Governor of the Punjab), nothing was done to evangelise the Gonds for some years. Then another godly civilian, Mr. Mosley Smith, Sessions Judge of Jubbulpore, in consultation with the Chaplain at Jubbulpore, obtained funds from the C.M.S. to support a German missionary, the Rev. J. W. Rebsch, sent by Pastor Gossner. He it was who started the once famous C.M.S. High School in Jubbulpore, which for many years did

F

such excellent work in the Central Provinces, not only for our Indian Christians, but for the sons of leading Hindu and Moslem families.   For a short period the Rev. E. C. Stuart, afterwards Bishop of Waiapu in New Zealand (and in very late life a missionary of the C.M.S. in Persia), was stationed in Jubbulpore and did some work among the Gonds.   Then came the Rev. E. Champion, who for twenty-one years pressed forward with great vigour the work in this region, and started an orphanage for boys rescued from famine near Mandla. Amongst the boys trained in this orphanage was Failbus (the Indian form of Philip) who was the first Indian clergyman ordained by me in 1904, and who did such fine work amongst the Gonds for many years.

After Mr. Champion retired he was succeeded by the Rev. E. D. Williamson, who laid the main foundations of our exist- ing work amongst the Gonds of this district.   The Gondi language was, under his guidance, reduced to writing and portions of the New Testament and numerous Bible stories were translated into Gondi.   He also baptised the first Gond convert, the head man of his village who had a great reputa- tion for religious devotion.   This Gond devotee, named Bhoi Baba, had learnt to read and used to spend long periods in meditation on a huge rock in the middle of a river.

Later on, after Mr. Williamson's departure, there came a remarkable missionary, the Rev. H. P. Parker, who not long after his arrival amongst the Gonds was appointed to succeed Bishop Hannington, the martyr Bishop of Uganda ; and who, as is well known, died of malaria before reaching his Diocese.

Hitherto no missionary had established himself in the heart of the country. When the Rev. Herbert Molony was appointed to this mission, he felt the time had arrived to launch into the depths of the jungle country, and he proceeded to establish himself at Marpha.   Here he was later on joined by a small body of lay evangelists, Herbert, Hack and others, and work was opened out in various villages.   Here he remained with his companions several years, doing all in his power to help the Gonds spiritually as well as physically.

At the time of his appointment as Secretary of the Mission

of the C.M.S. in my Diocese, he was living in Mandla with his sister, a devoted mission-worker, superintending the whole of the Gond Mission. In the winter of 1903 I paid this Mission my first visit. Together with Herbert Molony and my chaplain I rode across it from end to end, visiting the various mission stations, preaching in villages and holding confirmations. At Patpara, one of its principal stations, I found Mr. and Mrs. J. Fryer with a Boys' School, a Girls' School, an orphanage, and a small leper settlement under their care. Shortly after this I ordained Mr. Fryer to the Diaconate, and later on to the Priesthood. I also dedicated their Mission Church at Patpara under the rather suitable title of St. John in the Wilderness. Both Mr. and Mrs. Fryer have now passed to their rest. His little book, " The Story of the Gond Mission," tells in a simple and interesting way of the efforts which a body of devoted men and women have made to bring the Gonds to the knowledge of Christ. The peace of this settlement at Patpara was sometimes disturbed by wild animals. On one occasion Mr. Fryer and his flock were considerably alarmed by a man-eating panther which endeavoured to dig its way into some of the huts. Eventually the animal got into a fowl run, and before it was killed it had finished off a large number of the hens and chickens!

It was during this first long visit to this Mission in 1903 that I visited Karanjia, the scene of the tragedy of 1842. Here I found the grave of those four German missionaries in a deplorable state. The stone cross at the head of the grave had been maliciously broken by a Mohammedan fanatic. At my suggestion, Herbert Molony wrote a short pamphlet called " A Forgotten Tragedy," describing the death of these devoted men. Later on we took steps to have the grave repaired and placed a solid iron Maltese cross horizontally on the slab which covered the grave. On each arm of the cross is inscribed the name of one of the four missionaries : the Rev. Alois Loesch, Julius Schleisner, Karl Gatzky, and Heinrich Gossner. Underneath are written in Hindi the beautiful words, " Blessed are the dead which die in the Lord."

In this Gond Mission of the Mandla District I spent many

of the happiest days of my episcopate. Price, one of its well known missionaries, used to say that I was never quite myself till I was among them! I generally went there every cold weather. Patpara, Deori, its little agricultural settlement, and Marpha, were its most important stations. The district at that time was wild and primitive. There were few roads, and one had to ride from village to village across the jungle, largely guided by foot-tracks made by the villagers from one village to another. To save the expense of the transport of tents the Mission had erected several primitive rest houses with mud walls and either grass or tiled roofs, along the route which lay between Patpara and Marpha. They were very welcome after a long ride under a hot sun. Our food and bedding was carried either by coolies or pack ponies. In the remoter places we got camels if possible. On one tour with Price the camel drivers lost four of their baby camels, the last being carried off by a panther a few yards from our tent. In the rainy season, with practically no roads and two tributaries of the Nerbudda, the Halon and Burmeer, to cross, it was almost impossible for the missionaries at Marpha to get away as the rivers were often in flood and unbridged.

The Gond Mission has had a succession of very devoted missionaries who served it for longer and shorter periods during my episcopate. Some have passed to their rest, and some have retired from the field to work in quiet country parishes in England. Amongst those who are no longer with us, much the best known were the Rev. E. D. Price and his devoted wife. For many years they lived in the solitude of Marpha, contented and happy. Their two children, now missionaries, spent their earliest years in this solitude. Price, sometimes known as Tiger Price from his love and success in Shikar, though on one occasion he nearly lost his life when mauled very badly by a wounded panther (his life being saved by his fox terrier), was a man after the heart of the Gonds. He loved them and they loved him. He dearly loved organising the processions and "tamashas" which appealed to the primitive people. On one occasion when riding in one of these noisy processions with guns, drums and banners, we spied a herd of black buck two or three hundred yards away. Ordering the procession to proceed very slowly, he and I dismounted. A lucky shot from my too often erring rifle gave some excellent venison to the village, and within a few minutes we were riding on as if nothing had occurred.

For his excellent work in starting schools in the surrounding villages, and so promoting education among a people who did not seem over inclined for it, Price was awarded the Kaiser-i-Hind medal by Government. Before he left India he had raised money among his many friends to build a brick Church at Marpha. Many of us felt that a building more on the lines of the Gond dwellings would have been more suitable, but none of us had the heart to oppose an object so dear to the heart of one who had lived there all those years. We certainly did not envy the missionary who in future years was to keep it in repair! Of others who were there during my winter tours, and who invariably welcomed me and my wife, were the Rev. J. and Mrs. Wakeling, the Rev. J. and Mrs. Fleming, the Rev. F. D. O. and Mrs. Roberts, and the Rev. W. and Mrs. Hodgkinson. For a short time the late Rev. P. Proctor also worked in this Mission. All the wives of these missionaries were great workers amongst the Gond women, especially the late Mrs. J. Wakeling, and as they had a fair knowledge of medicine, were able to alleviate much suffering. Mr. and Mrs. Hodgkinson deserve a very special mention. He had started work in the Bhil Mission and had learnt the Bhil language, some time before that Mission was transferred to the Bombay Diocese. As I was very anxious for many reasons to secure his services in the Gond Mission, he volunteered for work in it, and the C.M.S. agreed to his transfer. The learning of a new language deterred neither him nor Mrs. Hodgkinson. He gave long years to working amongst the Gonds, and, in spite of serious trouble with his eyes owing to cataract, has been a fine example of courage and perseverance under great trials. The Rev. J. and Mrs. Fleming did excellent work during their comparatively short time at Marpha. For a good many years a devoted old couple, Mr. and Mrs. Charles, looked after the agricultural settlement at Deori. She has now gone to her rest, and he has retired in India.

Some mention must be made of the splendid work in Gond-
land of the Rev. F. D. O. Roberts. During his time in Marpha
there occurred serious scarcity amounting to famine.   Un-
deterred by many difficulties, Mr. Roberts organised, with the
assistance of the Government Forest Officers, both work and
food supplies for the starving people.   Useful tracks were converted into many miles of roads and necessary food was
brought into the wild country round Marpha.   For his services at this time Mr. Roberts was awarded the Kaiser-i-Hind
by Government.

Our leading Indian clergyman in the Gond country was the
Rev. Failbus, who brought out a grammar of the Gond
language.   During my episcopate we obtained two Indian
clergymen from the S.P.G. Mission in Chota Nagpur.   One of
them remained for but a short period, becoming home-sick
and finding life too hard; but the other, Joshua Khalko, was
willing to endure the loneliness and isolation of Marpha for
many years.   He sometimes confided in me that the Gonds
were far less willing to receive the Gospel message than the
Kols in Chota Nagpur.   On one occasion we invited him and
his wife to stay with us at Bishop's Lodge, Nagpur for a week
which they enjoyed intensely.

In spite of all the devotion and self-sacrifice of our missionaries it is still the day of small things in this Mission and only
seven or eight hundred Gonds have been baptised.   It is useless
to blind one's eyes to the plain fact that the number of our
missionaries at any given time in this wide stretch of wild
and roadless jungle country has almost always been far too
few, and that, from want of care, a good many Gond Christians in remote villages have relapsed into their old paganism.
Experience has taught us that when missions among aborigines
have grown into two or three thousand converts, difficulties
about marriage of daughters, a very real difficulty at times,
pass away, and the warm influences of Christian brotherhood
are felt.

That these Gonds are capable of feeling very strongly and
being attracted by leaders of their own race was brought home
to me years ago when I was touring in their country with my

Archdeacon, the Ven. Cyril Price, who is not to be confused with the Rev. E. D. Price to whom I have referred. A Gond who gave himself out to be " some great one " possessed of magical power drew a very large number of these people after him. While he was encamped near the Palace of the old Gond kings at Ramnagar, we found hundreds of Gonds gathered round him. He declined to allow us to see him, when we asked for an interview. We saw numbers of people bringing him all kinds of offerings, goats, young buffaloes and other things. We also saw a large number of his adherents, some quite old men and women, dancing frantically close to his large hut. We heard that he had rather a large harem and it was suggested that he had encamped near the Palace of the Gond kings with the idea of assuming the rôle of a Gond king, as well as a prophet. I learnt afterwards that the arrival of a body of police had the double effect of inducing him to leave Ramnagar, and of making the people return to their own villages. It is clear to me that, if some gifted Gond Christian in future days arises with a message to his race, one may see a big movement into the Christian Church. I am the more confirmed in this view when I recall what occurred in Chota Nagpur amongst the Kol aborigines forty years ago, when a clever, but half-instructed Christian, under discipline, gave himself out to be a prophet. Numbers of the simple aborigines being assured by him that the world was coming to an end and that only those who were with him would be saved, forsook the cultivation of their fields, and before the movement came to an end with his death, strong action had to be taken by Government.

They had, and I hope still have, an excellent custom in the Gond Mission, thoroughly in accord with Indian ideas, of holding " Melas " or religious gatherings, when the Gond Christians, scattered far and wide in different villages, assembled for a few days either at Diwari, near the Burmeer river, or Marpha, or Patpara near the Nerbudda river. The days were spent, as at Hindu Melas, with religious services and games, and meals together. If at Diwari or Patpara there was also some bathing. The religious addresses were often given by specially gifted missionaries, men and women, the Mission's ladies being invited to address the Gond women. There was a holiday atmosphere about it all, and a genuine feeling of kindliness. I remember how at one of the earlier Melas, the present Bishop of Madras, Harry Waller, took a leading part.

On one occasion when I had promised to attend a Mela at Diwari I was held up by heavy rain and was thirty miles from the gathering on Saturday night. As I had to conduct a confirmation at eleven o'clock on the Sunday morning, I had to get on my horse very early, and found a fresh horse from the Mission waiting for me half way. When I reached the river, however, I found it in flood and my flock on the opposite side! There were two small dugouts, or canoes, and placing a small plank between them I got my right leg into one and my left into the other, sitting on the connecting plank. All went well till I attempted to rise and get out, when the combination collapsed, and I was given a thorough ducking which amused my flock hugely, and did me no harm!

At another Mela it was decided to have a baby show, and as I had promised to give the prizes, I foolishly claimed the sole right to be the only judge, refusing the assistance of my wife and the other lady missionaries. Quite a number of Gond women brought their babies, some fat and lovely creatures, and some very pinched and tiny. When I saw the look of extreme anxiety on the part of the mothers as they presented to me their little darlings, my courage failed me, and whispering to each mother something of the beauty of her baby, I gave them all prizes!

Two specially interesting memories come back to me which I will record before concluding what I have to say about this Gond Mission. In 1910, when reports reached me that the Mission staff was so depleted that there was only one European missionary in the District, I determined to spend some time with him in visiting the different stations. As it was in the middle of the hot weather, when the sun's rays are very punishing, Mr. Wakeling and I determined to ride across the jungle by the light of the moon, and so avoid the heat. The

Indian moon sheds such a wonderful light that we found our way without much difficulty. At that time of the year one sees around one, especially in the wooded hills, a good many jungle fires which light up everything, and as far as I remember, our chief difficulty was experienced in getting our horses down the banks, and across the rocky bed of the river Halon. While we heard from time to time the weird calls of various animals, none disturbed us; but I will admit that when we got to the rest houses as day was breaking, I felt far more inclined to lie down and sleep than take the trouble of getting out of my riding kit.

The other memory was when Sadhu Sunder Singh visited Patpara to conduct a mission. I can still picture his tall commanding figure in his white robe, and his rapid and fervid addresses. My last sight of him was early in 1926 when he came to see me in Nagpur one afternoon. We talked and prayed together in my Chapel. He was a very fascinating person, quite unlike anyone I have ever seen. I used to say that I hoped he would never be spoilt by the open admiration which many, especially women, expressed for him. He was a decidedly mysterious person, and some of those who admired him greatly wondered whether his imagination did not run away with him, and make him think his imaginings were realities. Where is he now? His description of himself and of his conversion, given in a short article in our Nagpur Diocesan Magazine will interest those who have not read Canon Streeter's " Life of the Sadhu."

Sunder Singh was not a Christian all his life. He was born in 1889 in a wealthy Sikh family in north India. He says, " I was not a Sikh, but seeker after truth." Regarding his conversion, when sixteen years old, he says in his own words, " Preachers and Christians in general had often come to me and I used to resist them and persecute them. When I was out in any town I got people to throw stones at Christian preachers. I would tear up the Bible and burn it when I had a chance. In the presence of my father I cut up the Bible and other Christian books and put kerosine oil upon them and burnt them. I thought this was a false religion, and tried all

I could to destroy it. I was faithful to my own religion but I could not get any satisfaction or peace, though I performed all the ceremonies and rites of that religion. So I thought of leaving it all and committing suicide. Three days after I had burnt the Bible I woke up at about three o'clock in the morning, had my usual bath, and prayed, ' O God, if there is a God, wilt Thou show me the right way or I will kill myself.' My intention was that if I got no satisfaction, I would place my head upon the railway line when the five o'clock train passed by and kill myself. If I got no satisfaction in this life, I thought I would get it in the next. I was praying and praying but got no answer, and I prayed for half an hour longer hoping to get peace. At 4.30 a.m. I saw something of which I had no idea previously. In the room where I was praying I saw a great light. I thought the place was on fire. I looked around but could find nothing; then the thought came to me that this might be an answer that God had sent me. Then, as I prayed and looked, with the light I saw the form of the Lord Jesus. It had such an appearance of glory and love. If it had been some Hindu incarnation I would have prostrated myself before it. But it was the Lord Jesus Christ Whom I had been insulting a few days before. I felt that a vision like this could not come out from imagination. I heard a voice saying in Hindustani, ' How long will you persecute Me? I have come to save you. You were praying to know the right way, why do you not take it? ' The thought came to me, ' Jesus Christ is not dead, but living, and it must be He Himself.'

" So I fell at His feet and got this wonderful peace which I could not get anywhere else. This is the joy I was wishing to get. This was heaven itself. When I got up the vision had all disappeared, but although the vision disappeared the peace and joy have remained with me ever since."

The Sadhu has chosen Tibet as his principal field of work, as he regards the conversion of Tibet as a duty incumbent on the Indian Church. He tries to spend a part of each year there. In his journeys he has covered his own Punjab, Kashmir, Baluchistan and Afghanistan, South India and

Ceylon. He has visited Burma, the Straits Settlements, China and Japan, Europe, America and Australia. He has never identified himself with any denomination. He feels that by doing so restrictions and limitations would be imposed on his particular work. On the subject of Christian unity he remarks, " If Christians cannot live together happily here in this short life, how will they live together in eternity? The children of God are very *dear,* but very *queer.* They are very nice, but very narrow." Sunder Singh is a mystic, and our contemporary, but a mystic who appeals to our present age. His consciousness of a communion with God leads him to a life of unselfish activity; to a life devoted to the service of his fellow men.

This saintly Indian has not been heard of for some years and is now presumed to be dead.

(2) *The Bhil Mission of the C.M.S.*

Who are the Bhils?—The Tamer of these wild Bhils—His Missionary grandson—The first Missionary, his life and tragic death—The great famine in Bhil-land—Mission Stations at Lusaria, Billadia and Kherwara—Miss Bull, a great missionary—The Rev. A. I. and Mrs. Birkett—Tragic losses in Nissio—Tours in Bhil-land—Transfer to Bombay Diocese, 1916.

When we started our Nagpur Diocesan Chronicle in 1904, I appealed very strongly to all our clergy to make it a real success by contributing short articles regarding the history of their missions, or military cantonments or civil stations and out-stations. The result was that in all our earlier issues there was an immense amount of historical information about many places which aroused wide interest. Bishop Copleston told me at that time he considered our magazine was the most interesting of its kind in India. It is from an article by the Rev. Arthur Outram, grandson of the famous Sir James Outram, that I glean the earliest history of our mission to this aboriginal tribe.

Many of us have heard of the Indian schoolboy's answer to the question, " Who is the Bhil?" " The Bhil is a black man only blacker. If you meet him he shoots you from behind a tree, and throws your body in a ditch.   By this you may know the Bhil."

This aboriginal tribe was driven by the more civilised Aryans from Rajputana and Central India into the hilly country which extends from Udaipur to Khandesh. Never entirely conquered by the better armed Rajputs, they continued for centuries to live by ravaging and looting their more wealthy neighbours, retiring with their spoil into the then inaccessible jungle which covered these hilly tracts.   In 1818 the Bhils came within the sphere of British influence and some means had to be adopted to stop their daily dacoities and petty warfare which demoralised the surrounding country.   So in 1825 a British officer, Captain James Outram, was sent to " tame the Bhils." Having his quarters in Khandesh, he accomplished his task first by gaining their confidence, and then by forming his Bhil friends into armed police to keep their fellow Bhils in order.   After ten years' work the south part of the Bhil country in Central India and Khandesh was reduced to comparative law and order.   With the same object in view the British Government started the Mewar Bhil Corps in 1840 with its headquarters at Kherwara in the Mewar State of Rajputana, whose capital is at Udaipar.   Gradually the Bhils were induced to forsake dacoity and take to cultivating the land.   During the terrible famine of 1899—1900, the old spirit from time to time broke out and Bhils would raid grain merchants' shops and food caravans in their dire necessity.

Our Church's mission to these most interesting people owes its origin to the wife of one of the British officers of the Mewar Bhil Corps, Mrs. Rundall, daughter of the late Bishop of Exeter (Dr. Bickersteth), who was at Kherwara, the Corps headquarters, 115 miles from the nearest railway station.   She told her father in letters that the visits of their clergyman, the Government Chaplain of Neemuch, Central India, to the station were very infrequent, and asked him if he could possibly help them.   The result of his daughter's appeal led Bishop Bickersteth to approach the Church Missionary Society with a gift of £1,000 in order to start a mission to the Bhils and provide a clergyman for Kherwara.

In 1878 a charming little church and churchyard were completed and consecrated by Bishop Johnson, and in 1880 the Rev. C. J. Thompson was appointed by the Society to start his mission work among the Bhils. Here Thompson laboured for nearly twenty years. It was very uphill work and not till 1889 had he and the Rev. and Mrs. Collins, who were working with him, the joy of seeing their first converts baptised, an old man Sukha and his wife and family. Various helpers came for shorter or longer periods and then left, but Mr. Thompson continued. He was a man of fervent prayer who often withdrew for periods to devote himself to prayer.

In 1899 the Bhil country was visited by a terrible famine. Shortly before this the Rev. Arthur Outram, the grandson of the famous " Tamer of the Bhils " (General Sir James Outram of Mutiny fame), had arrived in the mission accompanied by his wife. The difficulty of getting food into these inaccessible hill tracts was so great, as roads in those days were few and far between, that in many places more than half the Bhil population lost their lives. At the time when the famine started Thompson was at home in poor health after his years of toil. Hearing of the growing sufferings of the Bhils and in spite of grave warnings from the doctors, he could not be prevailed on to stay away from these Bhils whom he loved. Toiling with Outram and several other missionaries who came from other parts of India to give their help (amongst them our present Metropolitan, Bishop Foss Westcott), Thompson was seized with a fatal attack of cholera, and died almost alone under a tree in the jungle. A large stone cross at Kalbai, ten miles from Kherwara, marks the spot where this apostolic man passed to his well-earned rest.

During the twelve years that this Mission remained in the Nagpur Diocese I endeavoured to visit it every year. There were two clerical missionaries and one lay missionary working in the Mission in 1903 when I paid my first visit, and two or three lady missionaries. The senior missionary at that time was the Rev. Arthur Outram. He had suffered very seriously from famine dysentery in 1900, and had been conveyed to Bombay in almost a dying condition. Returning in 1901 with the seeds of this trying sickness still lingering on, he was, to the regret of everyone and his own lasting sorrow and disappointment, compelled to leave India for good in 1904.

My first ride over that country was in his company when I first visited Lusadia, where Miss Bull and Miss Carter were at work with Mr. Vyse, the lay Missioner. We then rode on to Billadia, where the Rev. W. and Mrs. Hodgkinson and their two baby boys were stationed, and afterwards went on to Kherwara where the Mission originally started. There were at that time one or two hundred converts. One moved in an atmosphere of deep spiritual earnestness and prayer. Some of the earliest Bhil converts had been "Bhagats" or "devotees" in their non-Christian days and were looked up to by the other Christians.

The Bhils are a fine virile people, full of fun and good spirits. While Mr. Outram and I were riding one day near a Bhil village during the Hindu Festival of Holi (which I regret to say is not "holy" in our sense as it is a time of heavy drinking and debauchery), a group of Bhil women joining hand in hand endeavoured to stop us. They wanted the "sahibs" to give them money; they were quite ready to pull us off our horses to get it! Outram, knowing their little ways, galloped at them, when they dispersed amid shouts of laughter.

After Outram's breakdown in health there came from the Lucknow Diocese a really great missionary with his devoted and able wife, the late Rev. A. I. and Mrs. Birkett. Mrs. Birkett was a fully qualified doctor. Mr. Birkett, after taking his degree at Cambridge, had begun his career as an architect when the call came to follow Christ in the Mission Field. Not long after his ordination he was sent by the C.M.S. to Lucknow. Here he did splendid work, first as a leader of an evangelical band, and later on as an educational missionary. He designed and built, mostly at his own expense, a fine Boys' High School, which is still doing excellent work. Hearing of the serious plight in which the Bhil Mission was placed by the loss of Outram, he volunteered for work amongst the Bhils. It must have been a great wrench to him and his wife to leave such a highly civilised and charming station as Lucknow with all its interests and pleasant society, but they counted no sacrifice too great in following the Call which to them seems to have been always clear.

Travelling in the Bhil country was not altogether an easy matter. Apart from a long railway journey of nearly 1,000 miles, we had to put up with any and every kind of animal which could be found to carry us over a not good riding country. On one or two occasions I had lucky escapes from what might have been serious accidents. During those early years I dedicated two of the Churches of this Mission, one at Lusaria and one at Billadia. The Church at Lusaria was built almost entirely by the Bhils themselves without outside help save for the roof and tiles. The C.M.S. did not encourage consecration in their Mission Churches, owing largely I believe to the uncertainty of the tenure of the land. When I asked these Bhils, who built the Lusaria Church, to whom they wished it to be dedicated, they said at once, " Only to Christ."

In 1909 I ordained G. C. Vyse to the Diaconate at Christ Church, Lusaria, in the presence of a large number of the Bhil people amongst whom he had been working for a number of years. He was a great favourite with the Bhils and entered wholeheartedly into their lives. I remember seeing him one night taking part with a number of the Bhil men in a sword dance, under the light of the moon aided by a supply of torches. The Bhil Christians were particularly fond of composing Christian Bhagans, or hymns, and it was our regular practise to invite them up on certain evenings to sing their Bhagans either on the verandah of the Mission bungalow or at the Church.

Within a year of the transfer of the Bhil Mission to the Bombay Diocese, two great tragedies occurred which cast a widespread gloom in missionary circles in India. When returning from leave in March 1916, Miss Bull was drowned when the P. & O. SS. *Persia* was torpedoed by an enemy submarine off Crete. She was in every way a unique missionary, courageous and high-spirited, full of sympathy for the simplest and least attractive of the people in the district. Her personal devotion to our Lord and to His work could be read and marked by everyone.

And hardly had this tiny Mission begun to recover from this shock, when its leader, the Rev. A. I. Birkett, on his return from a holiday with his wife, was drowned on October 17th in a river in Bhilland. His horse either stumbled badly or came down in a flooded river, and unseated him. His right foot being caught in the stirrup, and his arms tightly closed in a waterproof cape, though a powerful swimmer, he was unable to swim. His Christ-like humility, his wonderful love and self-sacrifice for the simple Bhils, his simplicity of life, and his evangelistic zeal, will never be forgotten by those who were fortunate enough to know him. During his years in the Mission the Bhil Church had grown considerably. A great French Abbé has said, " only sacrifice is fruitful." Can we doubt but that some day those lives given so willingly and completely to Christ for the extension of His Kingdom will bear abundant fruit amongst these interesting children of the jungle.

(3) *The Chanda Mission of the Scottish Episcopal Church*

An Indian Chaplain responsible for starting the Mission—Father Nehemiah Goreh one of its first missionaries—The Rev. Israel Jacob works in Chanda for twenty years—Arrival of the Rev. Alex Wood, 1898—Is joined by the Rev. G. D. Philip—Early work in mission—Consecration of St. Andrew's Church in City—Lady workers—Arrival of Rev. J. R. McKenzie, B.D.—Alex Wood consecrated Bishop of Chota Nagpur, 1920—Later Missionaries—The Rev. Mackenzie, M.D.M.C., D.S.O.—Annual visits and delightful tours in Chanda District.

It is interesting to note that the Mission at Chanda, like more than one mission of our Church in India, owes its commencement to an Indian Chaplain. In the year 1870, when Chaplain of Nagpur, the Rev. G. T. Carruthers first urged the claims of India on the Episcopal Church of Scotland. Hitherto that Church had directed its foreign missionary efforts almost exclusively to work in South Africa. The earlier efforts of the Chanda Mission were carried on largely by Indian workers. For a time the saintly Father Nehemiah Goreh, commonly called " Nilkant Shastri," a converted Maratha Brahmin, worked in Chanda. It was my good fortune to meet this remarkable man in Allahabad in January

1892. It was at the Magh Mela held at the confluence of India's two great rivers, the Ganges and Jumna. Thousands of Hindu pilgrims were there, and hundreds of Sadhus, Sanyasis, and religious mendicants of all types. There in the midst of them moved this Christian Brahmin with a countenance on which the peace of God was stamped. I appreciate deeply Bishop Wood's description of Nehemiah Goreh's work and influence in Chanda in early days, given in his charming little book " In and Out of Chanda." He writes : " The story I like best of all is how he used to preach in the bazaar. They tell of him as a slim figure dressed in a white cassock. Round his neck was a rosary of wooden beads and attached to it a wooden cross. In his hand he held a heavy wooden cross, that stood higher than his head, and on this he leaned. People passed and repassed going about their business, but he stood still, taking no notice of them whatever. But as he stood there for an hour perhaps, or more, the people noted, watched, stood around at a distance, waiting shyly, for whether he were a Christian or not, at least he was a Brahmin. Then, at last when a circle had gathered round him in the cool of the evening, he preached to them of Christ." Under his saintly influence the Mission grew, and when he left Chanda in 1874 he had already gathered out from heathenism a small body of Christians. Then for twenty years the Mission was entrusted to the care of the Rev. Israel Jacob, until the arrival of the Rev. Alex Wood in December 1898.

Shortly after his arrival in India, more than thirty-five years ago, Alex Wood visited the Dublin University Mission at Hazaribagh, Chota Nagpur, of which I was then Head. Neither of us then dreamt that in a few years we should become fellow-workers for many years, in the then unformed Diocese of Nagpur, I as its first Bishop, from 1903—26, and he as my successor in 1926. His early years as a missionary must have been extremely lonely and uphill. He had no companion missionary till the Rev. G. D. Philip arrived three years later. Within less than a year of his arrival this and other parts of India were visited by a terrible famine, and Wood was called upon to supervise two famine labour camps where a large number of famine-stricken were employed in making a road to the south of the district. Mounted on his old white horse Eli (so called from its habit of rearing!), with his white dog Potiphar, he was visiting one of the labour camps when he surprised three or four big Pathans (up-country Mohammedans from the frontier) trying to get the key of the money safe from the Bengali overseer who kept it. He found them trying to roast the man over a frying pan! His method of dealing with these sinners was one which only a very powerful man could have carried out successfully. He was both their judge and executioner; and after a very severe chastisement they left the camp in sorrow of heart, and achings of body, but with a lasting respect for this young padre sahib, who instead of sending them to jail punished them himself!

Within a fortnight of my consecration in March 1903 I paid the first of many visits to this interesting Mission. It is the one strong point of contact between the Scottish Episcopal Church and the Church of India. It was always very near the heart and in the prayers of the saintly Bishop Wilkinson, Primus of the Scottish Episcopal Church. He it was who sent Wood to Chanda, their first missionary to India. Shortly before my first visit the Rev. G. D. Philip had arrived out from Scotland, and two lady workers, Miss Smith and Mrs. Aitken, had joined the staff.

Few Missions in India have quite such picturesque surroundings as the headquarters of this Mission, and few have a more trying climate. The Mission bungalow with the Girls' Orphanage and small hospital are just outside the old Gond city of Chanda, with its beautiful red-stone walls of Saracenic architecture, its tombs of the Gond kings, and some interesting temples. During my first visit Wood took me to call on the descendant of the old Gond Rajah who was very anxious for me to visit the tombs of his ancestors. His own dwelling was such a contrast to their splendour, and his tiny grand-daughter so entirely devoid of clothing that I ventured to suggest to a Government official that a small addition to his pension would be a gracious act on the part of Government. I believe my remark was taken seriously and something more was given him. We must remember that it was the Mahratta Bhonsla Rajah who had deposed his ancestor and not the British!

During my second visit to Chanda, eight months later, I consecrated the Mission Church of St. Andrew in the heart of the city. The Boys' Boarding School was also in the city. I ought to add that there had been a Church outside the city for many years for the English residents, dedicated to St. Jude.

I have so many pleasant and interesting memories connected with Chanda during my frequent visits extending over twenty-three years that I can only give a general idea of the kind of work they are doing and aiming at doing in this district and select some few events which still stand out clearly. There is the work at headquarters and the work just outside Chanda and in the district. The staff has never been a strong staff numerically, but it has had amongst its numbers workers of great devotion and real ability. Miss Smith and Miss Rowell among the earlier lady workers are names that will never be forgotten. Miss Smith, before she came to Chanda, had been working under Bishop Frank Weston in the Universities Mission to Central Africa, till her health broke down and she was ordered out of Africa never to return. India has treated her, as far as health is concerned, more kindly, for though she has passed through many sorrows, first losing her only child, then her husband, Canon Philip, and still later a very dear adopted Indian daughter, Tulsi (who was drowned at a picnic), she still lives on in Jubbulpore helping in the work of the Church in every way she can. Later on Miss Woodcock and Miss Olive Flint joined the staff and are still bravely and faithfully doing all in their power to commend the Gospel of our Lord to the women of Chanda.

In 1909 the staff was still further strongly strengthened by the arrival from Scotland of the Rev. J. R. McKenzie, B.D. He was then in Deacon's orders, and was ordained priest by me two years later in our Cathedral at Nagpur. It was his arrival in Chanda which made it possible for the Mission to open out its branch in Nagpur where Canon Philip and his wife (formerly Miss Smith) did such valuable work both for the Indian Christian community and by starting the Anglo-Indian Home.   In 1919 McKenzie accepted a professorship at the Edinburgh Theological College, but when Alex Wood, who was Head of the Mission, was offered the Bishopric of Chota Nagpur and felt he could not accept it while his Mission was so understaffed, McKenzie resigned his professorship and returned to Chanda as Head of the Mission.   There he worked till 1931 when the education of his two sons compelled him, greatly to everyone's regret, to return to Scotland. He was awarded the Kaiser-i-Hind gold medal by Government for his public services in Chanda, and for his Boy Scout work, some years before he retired.

Of those later workers with whom I came most in contact there is one to whom I feel I must refer.   In 1911 when I was visiting Scotland during my leave I was introduced at the Cathedral in Dundee to Dr. Kenneth Mackenzie who had been for some years in the Indian Medical Service.   He had felt a Call to Holy Orders, and though married, had resigned his commission and was then preparing for ordination. Shortly after his ordination to the Diaconate, war had broken out, and he at once joined up as a doctor, and served four years in France.   For his war services he had been awarded the M.C. and Bar, and later on the D.S.O.   He was ordained priest in 1919 and made Rector in Lanark.   Hearing that Chanda was seriously understaffed he came out for two years, 1921—3, throwing himself heart and soul into the work.   For a time he lived in a hut in the little village of Durgapur, three miles from Chanda, to help its small Christian community.   Chanda has again attracted him, for after some years in Scotland, he has returned to the Mission with his wife and daughters.

One of the most delightful experiences in a good many years were tours in the Chanda jungles with either Alex Wood or Roddy McKenzie.   My wife and I would send out horses either by road or train the hundred miles from Nagpur to Chanda, and for a fortnight or three weeks of a glorious Indian winter move along through the splendid forest country, camping outside large villages and having meetings in the evenings.   We frequently used the magic lantern.   I generally

CONSECRATION OF ST. THOMAS' MISSION CHURCH : NAGPUR, 1925

had an interpreter, one of the catechists or an Indian clergy-man, as the villagers further south did not understand Hindi.

On one of our tours with Alex Wood while we were seated at breakfast in a forest bungalow, a deputation came from a village some miles off to tell us that a tiger had killed two bullocks the day before and asking us to come to their assist-ance. We rode over after breakfast and, leaving our horses near the village, took up our positions about mid-day. Wood, who was a fine rifle shot (he had shot for the Indian team at Bisley), most unselfishly gave me the position where it was most probable the tiger would come out from the jungle. Seated in the " machan " with my wife who was knitting, I fell asleep only to be awakened by the approaching noise of the beaters. Greatly to my delight a magnificent tiger came out just where I wanted it and I killed him with my first shot.

In 1925 a great sorrow descended upon the Mission, when Canon G. D. Philip, after a long and most trying illness, consequent upon an operation, passed onward into fuller light. I have seldom met anyone who lived more in the spirit than did this saintly kindly man.

In 1925 the Primus of the Scottish Church visited us, accompanied by Mrs. Robberds. I had for many years asked him to come out to India and spend a couple of months with us during the cold weather, and at length the way was clear for him to accept the invitation. He and Mrs. Robberds spent some time with us in Nagpur, and then paid an extensive visit to the Mission in Chanda, going down to the south of that district and seeing the primitive Gonds in their villages. One evening they saw a large number of the most jungly men and women dancing one of their dances with torches lighting up this weird scene. Certainly the Maria Gonds in South Chanda are a much wilder and more primitive people than the Gonds of the Mandla district, where the C.M.S. are working. Amongst the many services rendered to us by the Primus during his visit was a beautiful sermon at the consecration of the new Mission Church of St. Thomas in Nagpur. It was virtually a memorial Church to the late Canon G. D. Philip. He had set his heart on the building of this Church and had raised much of the money needed for it.   I have never forgotten one sentence in the Primus' sermon when speaking on the need of the consecration of our lives, "A consecrated Church and an unconsecrated people are not pleasant to contemplate."

I remember with peculiar pleasure the ordinations of some of the Indian clergy of this Mission.   They were good, simple fellows, in whom the Mission had every confidence.   The first in December 1908 was Habaji Bhalerao, who served a long diaconate, being ordained to the priesthood seven years later. The second was in 1910, Whadarashta Samuel Silas, who having served a five years' diaconate was ordained priest in 1915.   The third was in 1914, Suwartik Sudoba Jadhav, who was ordained priest three years later.   The fourth and fifth were in 1921, Samuel Gopal Patwardhan and Habil Jagtap, who were ordained priests some years later.   My last ordination before I returned in February 1924, was when I ordained Balwant Rao Salve to the Diaconate.   It was to me a very real joy when I resigned the Bishopric of Nagpur in 1926, that my successor was Alex Wood, the former Head of this Mission.

CHAPTER VIII

(1) *Jubbulpore and Katni*

Great changes in India during the last thirty years—Politics for a time
absorb the thought of the educated—A great contrast between Pertap
Chander Mozoomdar 1894 and Mahatma Gandhi 1932—The work in
Jubbulpore—Some of its well known Missionaries—A delegation of the
C.M.S. visits the Mission after the war—Serious reduction of staff for
financial reasons—The Church of England Zenana Mission in Jubbulpore
and District—Katni a bright spot in our mission work.

THERE is a great deal of difference between the missionary
work in the jungle country where the aboriginal Gonds and
Bhils are living, and in large towns like Jubbulpore and
Nagpur.   When I began my missionary life in India as long
ago as January 1892, there was among the educated and
student class in India a real keenness to hear and learn what
the Gospel message had for them.   I remember how a few
days after I arrived in Calcutta in January 1892 with my
brothers of the Dublin University Mission, and was staying
with the Oxford University Mission in Calcutta before going
up country, we heard the late Father Brown addressing a large
body of Calcutta University students on the Christian faith.
We heard, too, of many who were enquiring about the claims
of Christ.   There was at that time a strong feeling amongst
educated Hindus that Keshub Chander Sen's appeal to abolish
caste, idolatry, child marriage and the prohibition of re-
marriage of widows was fundamentally sound. I can remember
listening to lectures delivered by Babu Bepin Chander Pal on
the reform of the Hindu religion.   Everything then pointed
to an underlying " hunger and thirst for the true knowledge
of God."   And then, as the years passed on, politics became
more and more the absorbing thought of the Indian mind, and
amongst the educated classes everything else including religion
seemed to take a second place.   It seemed strange to me that

the same Babu Bepin Chander Pal who had spoken to me of his great desire that he and his children should be zealous missionaries for God and the truth, and see India rid of its evil customs of caste, idolatry, child marriage, etc., should have become some years later one of the keenest and most dangerous agitators against British rule, and ready to attribute all India's degradation and misfortune to British influence!

In a fairly long life in India which beginning in 1892 finished in 1926, one must expect to see great changes, but I cannot better illustrate how great that change has been than by recalling two speeches I listened to by two very distinguished Indians. The first of these speeches was delivered in 1894 in the Keshub Hall, Hazaribagh, Chota Nagpur. The speaker was Pertap Chander Mozoomdar, the Head of the New Dispensation. He was a successor of the Hindu reformer, Keshub Chander Sen. In the course of a speech on the need of vast reforms in Hinduism he said, " The best day that had ever dawned for India was the day the British came there." Few to-day remember, I fear, his brilliant book " The Oriental Christ." The other speech was delivered in the Church House, Westminster, in 1932, and the speaker was the Mahatma Gandhi. The Chairman was the Archbishop of York, and the audience was composed entirely of people of a religious and non-political character. One remark of the Mahatma's impressed me deeply and had I not felt it would be out of place to rise and contradict him, I would certainly have done so. The remark was, " The English think they have done a great deal of good in India, and we Indians don't, and we are the best judges." When one recalls what India was in the days when the British began to trade with it, the bloody invasions from the North-West Frontier, the terrible recurrent famines through the failure of the monsoons, the great strife between Rajput and Mahratta, the dark and cruel superstitions of " sati," infanticide, Thuggism, and human sacrifice, and what India is to-day, one can but see how racial prejudice and a growing national pride can blind even good men, like the Mahatma, to what England has done for India.

While there is, however, this great change of attitude

among the educated Indians of the cities and large towns, there is another change going on in India amongst millions of its people which is full of encouragement to those who long to see the Kingdom of our Lord Jesus Christ grow, and abound in that great country. Let me explain this by the contrast between forty years ago and to-day. It was my lot to spend my earliest years in India as a missionary in the jungle country of Chota Nagpur. In the south of the district of Hazaribagh, many thousands of the aborigines had become Christians; in the north the people were caste bound and unresponsive. To-day in the central and southern portions of Chota Nagpur, the Christians, Anglicans, Lutherans and Romans number several hundred thousand. In the district of Hazaribagh to the north, where I was working, caste held sway and the response was very slight. I remember how one evening I had been preaching for an hour outside a village, using the magic lantern with slides describing our Saviour's life, when the head man rose up and quite politely addressed me as follows :—" Padre Sahib, your religion is a very good religion, and our religion is a very good religion, and your religion is very good for you, and our religion is very good for us." Having said this he and my audience of about 100 villagers withdrew, leaving me and the Catechist alone. I often thought in those days of the words, " Master, we have toiled all the night and have taken nothing." And when I recall the meagre response to our efforts in those days with the wonderful awakening in the Mass Movement areas in various parts of India to-day, which are bringing hundreds of thousands of the poor into the Church of Christ, and through them numbers of the higher caste Hindus, one can really thank God and take fresh courage.

Our Mission work in the town of Jubbulpore and its sur-rounding country is of long standing. For a long period it was the only non-Roman Catholic Mission in this part and had a really strong staff of English missionaries. Both the Church Missionary Society and the Church of England Zenana Mission were co-operating in the work. They had a nice congregation of Indian Christians, and it was always a great pleasure to me to be invited to take part in the Sunday services and help in the preaching. In my early days the Sunday services were held in the Church of St. Luke in the heart of the town, but later on the late Canon Ernest Hensley, to save the majority of the Indian Christians as well as the European missionaries either long and fatiguing walks, or the expense of tongas, raised the money and built the beautiful Church of St. Paul's in the centre of the very fine C.M.S. property in Belbagh. In those days there was a really flourishing Indian Christian High School for boys in the town, and I well recall the time the late Rev. J. Challis acted as its Principal and Mr. Basu, an Indian, as its Head Master; and later days when the Rev. F. E. Keay acted as Principal and Mr. Modak as Head Master. It was to all of us a sore grief that an institution which had done such fine educational work for sixty years, had to be abandoned by the C.M.S. for lack of funds, though I believe it is now being carried on privately by a son of the late Mr. Modak.

Our Jubbulpore Mission, during its life which covers more than two generations, has had a number of very devoted and gifted C.M.S. missionaries. Three of them were called away to Bishoprics; Stuart to New Zealand, Molony to China, and Hope Gill to Travancore, South India. Among those with whom I was brought most closely into contact was the late Ernest Hensley who became one of the first three canons of our Cathedral. He was a fine linguist who could preach equally well in English and Hindustani, and he and his devoted wife did a really great work amongst the Indian Christians in Jubbulpore as well as their evangelistic efforts among the non-Christian Hindus and Moslems. Other excellent missionaries in this area were the Rev. E. Walker and Hamilton Blackwood, both of whom had to leave India owing to failing health. The Rev. R. Hack worked for some years at Katni until the Great War. During the War he spent long periods in France and German East Africa as a chaplain to the troops, and after the War, to everyone's regret, he did not return to India, largely, I believe, for health reasons.

After the War when the finances of the C.M.S. were

strained to breaking point, a delegation of that Society, in which their General Secretary, the Rev. Cyril Bardsley, now Bishop of Leicester, and their Indian Secretary, the late Canon Wigram, were the principal figures, visited Jubbulpore, and for a time it seemed likely that they would have to withdraw all their English missionaries from this area. I remember how I pointed out to them as forcibly as I could that to do so would be almost to extinguish the one missionary light which the Church of England had in this part of India!

A suggestion was then made that the Scottish Episcopal Church, who were working in Chanda, might possibly be able to take over the Jubbulpore Mission, but after much discussion and long correspondence the leaders of the Scottish Mission felt that their joint responsibilities in South Africa and Chanda made it impossible for them to face this increase in finance and staff. Finally, the C.M.S. authorities agreed to keep one English missionary in Jubbulpore for a period to carry on their work in that area, and to act as secretary and superintendent for all their Missions in the Diocese.

Their first missionary to come under these conditions was the Rev. J. Warren, a contemporary of mine at Dublin University. He had retired from India some years before after long years of service in Jubbulpore and Benares, and was acting as one of the C.M.S. secretaries in England. His volunteering to leave his wife and family and come when no longer young, and certainly not robust, lest the work should suffer, filled us all with the deepest admiration. When he was called away to higher service within four months of his return to India there were few who did not feel deeply moved by the self-sacrifice of this man " who loved not his life for Christ's sake that he might finish his course with joy." Since then the Rev. Canon J. Robinson has, for ten years, single-handed, carried on the work in Jubbulpore, with the general approval of everyone. When he retires, as he soon must, I can only hope that the C.M.S. may be able to send an equally devoted and capable man to take his place.

I must now say a few words about the Church of England Zenana Mission in Jubbulpore and Katni who co-operate with the C.M.S. in that area. I remember how on several occasions our late Metropolitan, Bishop Copleston, spoke to me with great admiration of the work of the Church of England Zenana Missionary Society in India. He spoke of the saintly women who carried it on, of their quiet unostentatious way of working, of the great affection shown by them to their Indian workers, and the children in their schools, which seemed to be fully reciprocated. I can only say how clearly, during my twenty-three years' episcopate, I saw the truth of what he said. The work of the C.E.Z.M.S. in Jubbulpore was built up for over thirty years by a really remarkable woman, Miss Elizabeth Branch. When she died in Pachmarhi a few years after she had retired from active work, her many friends and admirers erected a beautiful window in Christ Church, Pachmarhi, in her memory. She was succeeded by an Irish-woman of great devotion and discernment, the late Miss Christina Hall. When I lived in Jubbulpore, one of her lieutenants and fellow workers was Miss Florence Peddar, who won golden opinions from everyone by her work during one of our plague epidemics. Called away from India for family reasons, she worked as hard in England for the Mission as she had done in India, and since her father's death has returned to the sphere where she was so well known and loved twenty years previously. Another worker in the Jubbulpore area for the last twenty years or more has been Miss Eleanor Kirby, who has carried on the fine traditions of those devoted ladies of bygone days. Like the C.M.S. they have often had to face heavy financial reductions, which have necessitated the closing of a number of small schools and handing over some work to the American Mission.

I shall never forget how, about thirty years ago, in 1905, these devoted ladies were summarily evicted from their Mission House near Christ Church, Jubbulpore, by their Hindu land-lord because one of their pupils, a Hindu woman, became a Christian. It turned out, however, to be a blessing in disguise, for we were able to find a nice piece of land near the C.M.S. property on which was built the present Mission House.

But while our Anglican mission work in Jubbulpore itself

has suffered heavily through straitened finances owing to the Great War, and work that we might have done has been taken over by two well staffed American Missions, the Methodist Episcopal and Disciples of Christ, our C.E.Z.M.S. work in Katni has had a constant record of progress. There under the inspiring zeal and leadership of Deaconess Jane Bardsley, ably assisted by Miss Short, a small Indian Christian Girls' School has grown into a really fine Girls' High School where over 200 Indian Christian girls are receiving a splendid education to fit them for great usefulness in the land of their birth. It was one of the real privileges of my work in India to ordain Miss Jane Bardsley, a sister of the present Bishop of Leicester, to the office of a Deaconess of the Church. The work which she did in her school and outside it in Katni will never be forgotten. She also did valuable work on several of our Diocesan Boards. Since she retired, her place as Principal of this school has been taken by Miss Sophie Levi, for many years Head of the Government Training College for teachers in Jubbulpore.

I cannot conclude this little bundle of memories without referring to the Indian clergy whom I ordained in this Mission. One of them, the first I ordained, was Henry Sameida, who worked for a good many years in Katni and then in Jubbulpore. He was a man of sound ability with a deeply Christian character. I always felt he was a man of peace, and I know that when he passed to his rest a few years ago, everyone felt his loss deeply. In 1913 I ordained Pakkianatham Jacob, a Tamil by race, for work amongst the Tamil Christians in Jubbulpore. Some years later he left us for work in Singapore at the invitation of Bishop Ferguson Davie. It was a larger sphere of work, for the Tamils are among the most educated people in India and love to see what the rest of the world is like. Jacob was a keen evangelist with a most child-like faith, and I was deeply grieved when I heard of his rather early death. The next I ordained was the Rev. Uzziel David Theophilus, who had been trained at Bishop's College, Calcutta, our principal Theological College in India. He has been highly educated and is a man of real ability, and I have every hope he may render valuable work for many years. The two other Indian clergy whom I ordained for this Mission were both of them catechists of long standing and approved character. Their names were decidedly biblical, Mark Gideon, and Andrew George. Andrew George has an interesting history, for he was adopted when a small boy by a famous C.M.S. missionary, the Rev. Brocklesby Davies, who laboured at Benares and elsewhere in that part of India for over fifty years. He was the child of many prayers. Miss Davies, the daughter of the Rev. Brocklesby Davies, was present at the ordination of her adopted Indian brother and was, needless to say, overjoyed at the happy event. The Rev. Mark Gideon, since his ordination, has worked for many years in our Mission at Bharatpar, a native state in Rajputana, and is now working in Jubbulpore. He has proved himself a worthy and reliable pastor.

(2) *Bharatpur in Rajputana*

An interesting State in Rajputana—The Jats a virile race of people—The City and Fortress of Bharatpur—How our Mission was started—A day of small beginnings but full of hope.

About thirty miles to the west of Agra lies the capital of the Bharatpur State, a walled city eight miles in circumference. The people of this state are mainly Jats supposed by some to be of Scythian origin, the results of an invasion of former days, but regarded by Tod as of Rajput stock. The Jats, whatever be their remote origin, belong to one of the " fighting " races of India, and in addition to the State army of about ten thousand, a large number are recruited for our Indian Army. The city of Bharatpur is decidedly imposing, and its huge walls of mud and brick and a surrounding moat made it almost impregnable in ancient days. While the British were at war with Bharatpur in 1804, General Lake failed in his assaults on the city, but in 1827, Lord Combermere, Commander in Chief and afterwards a Field Marshal, by draining the moat succeeded in taking it by storm. The country around Bharatpur and indeed throughout the whole state is very fertile, and the Jats are good cultivators. The famous

Water Palaces at Dig, about twenty miles from the capital, are very beautiful, and I have often wondered why more cold weather visitors to India do not go and see them.

The history of our Mission work in this state is interesting. It arose out of a visit of one of the Oxford Mission to Calcutta, Father Walker, to Colonel Herbert, the Political Officer in this State. Colonel Herbert spoke of the very occasional visits they had of a chaplain or missionary from Agra, and wished that they might have them more frequently. The idea was then suggested that possibly they might get one of the Church Missionary Society's missionaries to care for the European Christians and also to do evangelistic work amongst the non-Christians. Just about the time a wealthy supporter of the C.M.S., hearing of this idea, gave a large sum to meet initial expenses of a building for the missionary, etc., and as the State offered no objection to this idea, the work was started.

The first missionary who was sent by the C.M.S. was the late Rev. J. M. Paterson. He and his wife were ideally suited for this early work which needed much sanctified common sense and tact. They realised that they must start quietly and win confidence before they could hope to accomplish much. They soon became friendly with everyone, including the State officials and the Maharajah himself. Mr. Paterson had been a very young officer in the Royal Artillery when the Call came to him to be a missionary of the Cross. After the usual period at the University he came out to work at Agra. He had paid occasional visits to Bharatpur before taking up his residence there, and I have no doubt that the fact that he was a very fine shot, and had on occasions much the largest bag at the famous Bharatpur winter duck shoots, made the Maharajah always look with friendly eyes on this rather unusual English padre ! Perhaps I ought to explain that surrounding the city of Bharatpur are a very large number of shallow lakes which are visited every cold weather by hundreds of thousands of wild duck from the hinterland of the Himalayas. One of the Political officers in Bharatpur told me that the noise of the various flights of these ducks on arriving at Bharatpur resembled the noise of an arriving train !

Four years after my first visit to Bharatpur, where I had several times spent delightful days with the Patersons, he was compelled for family reasons to withdraw from the mission field, and for a time his place was taken by the Rev. Hamilton Blackwood. During the early period of our Mission work in Bharatpur, Miss Bertha Fowler, a friend of Mrs. Paterson's, came out to visit her during the cold weather. So interested was she in the work that she determined to make it her life's work. To her this little Mission owes more than one can well describe. She gave freely and liberally of her substance to provide it with what it needed. A fine bungalow for the lady worker of the C.E.Z.M.S. was built at her expense, which later on she presented to that Society. Later on she herself lived in Agra in a Christian Girls' School which she helped to develop, but her interest in Bharatpur never ceased. Her home-call came to her when on her way to England in Egypt not many years ago. Those who, like myself, knew her fairly intimately, can never forget her intense kindness and devotion. For a period Miss Davies did good work in Bharatpur till she was transferred to the United Provinces. After Mr. Hamilton Blackwood's breakdown in health, the Rev. F. D. O. Roberts was stationed for some years at Bharatpur, but when financial stringency compelled the C.M.S. to withdraw their European clerical missionary, one of our Indian clergy, the Rev. Mark Gideon, was sent to take his place. He has laboured there for many years, but I understand that quite recently he has changed places with the Rev. Andrew George, he having been sent to Jubbulpore and Andrew George to Bharatpur. For many years past Miss Violet Saunders of the Church of England Zenana Mission has been working in Bharatpur, and her circular letters which from time to time have been sent to me have been most interesting. There seems to be a real spiritual movement going on amongst some of the people which encourages us to hope for a definite response to the efforts of the last thirty years.

(3) *Ajmeer in Rajputana*

The chief city of the British Enclave in Rajputana—A city regarded as
sacred by Mohammedans and Jains—The looting of the Deeg—The Jain
religion—The S.P.G. Mission—The Rev. Tara Chand—The late Mr.
Fordham—The Rev. Wilfred Jacob.

Ajmeer is, as I have already said, a place of great importance in Rajputana from a political point of view, being the
Headquarters of the chief British official in Rajputana. It is
also held in high regard by two of the seven religious bodies in
India, the Mohammedan and Jain. Many years ago, in 1780,
there came to Ajmeer a Mohammedan Fakir with a great
reputation for sanctity. There he lived for a time and there
he died. Pilgrimages are made to his tomb, and once a year
a weird and almost savage ceremony takes place near his
tomb, when a large cauldron containing many hundreds of
gallons is filled with food and beggars from far and wide come
to be fed. The " looting the deeg " as it is called, is a very
revolting scene, when there is a fierce scramble for the contents
of the cauldron. Of course, the feeding of beggars is in full
accord with the demand of Hindu and Mohammedan piety.
The Jains also regard Ajmeer as one of their sacred spots for
they have there a splendid temple, maintained by a number of
wealthy Jain merchants. I had first come in touch with the
Jain religion in my early missionary days. Mount Paresh-
nath in Chota Nagpur is their sacred mountain; and they
have some very fine temples on it. Very little missionary work
has been done amongst the Jains. Their religion arose about
the same time as Buddhism, but it has never drawn a large
number of persons with it, though it still holds its ground in
India. One of its chief tenets is the sacredness of all life. A
Jain would think it a sin to literally kill a flea. Some very
strict Jains keep a net over their mouths to prevent them from
destroying tiny insect life. Close to Ajmeer there is the sacred
Pushka lake around which cluster various Hindu temples.
One of these temples is dedicated to Brahma, the Creator,
who with Vishnu, the Preserver, and Shiva, the Destroyer,
form the Hindu Triad; the chief of India's multitude of gods
and goddesses. Professor Monier Williams suggests that here

H

alone in all India is Brahma the Creator really worshipped. It seems strange that while thousands of temples are dedicated to Vishnu, the Preserver, and Shiva, the Destroyer, there are only three or four temples in all India dedicated to Brahma the Creator. Why this is so, one does not really know. I remember speaking to the chief Brahmin priest at Pushka about it, but he obviously did not wish to discuss it. One view is that the Creator having done his work has left everything to Vishnu and Shiva; and like the God of Epicurus, sits in his Olympus lost in contemplation. The other view is that the Creator once sinned, and this no educated Hindu likes to mention. Our mission work in Ajmeer was started many years ago when the Rev. Tara Chand was sent there from the S.P.G. Mission at Delhi. He was the son of a well-to-do Hindu banker and was in Delhi as a boy during the Indian Mutiny. The conversion of his professor to Christianity made a deep impression on him, and later on he came under the influence of that really great missionary, Bishop Valpy French, the first Bishop of Lahore. Tara Chand was a very highly educated man, a Christian through and through. He was universally respected by Europeans and Indians alike. He was the author of several books in Urdu on the Faith.

We had in Ajmeer in addition to the beautiful station Church of St. Mary's, where the Europeans worship, a nice little Church dedicated to St. John in the heart of the city where the Indian Christians usually worship. I sometimes arranged that our Indian candidates for confirmation should be confirmed along with our English candidates at St. Mary's to emphasise our oneness in Christ. Near St. John's were a residence for our missionary and a stone house which had been built by Mr. Fordham, an Anglo-Indian, for an Orphanage. He had left a small endowment for this Orphanage, but as this was far too small to enable us to pay a matron as well as to clothe and board the orphans, I got his permission, before he died, to use the house for a day school and to use his endowment for the education of poor Anglo-Indian children. I remember how highly the late Bishop Johnson spoke of Mr. Fordham's generosity and his genuine anxiety to help the poor of the Community.

When it was obvious that Tara Chand's health was failing I ordained a young Indian with a Durham Degree, the Rev. Ethelred Judah, to assist him and to eventually take his place. Unfortunately, Ethelred Judah's health broke down and I then ordained the Rev. Wilfrid Jacob to take charge of this little Mission. Jacob had been trained by the Cambridge Mission at Delhi, and since his ordination has worked very faithfully and conscientiously in Ajmeer. There are besides our little Mission a Roman Catholic Mission, many of whose clergy are Franciscans, a strong Scottish Presbyterian Mission, and a Mission of the American Methodist Episcopal Church. The latter has a sanatorium for consumptives in another part of Rajputana. The special importance of our little S.P.G. Mission is, I have always felt, that it shepherds a number of Indian Christians, members of our Church, engaged in railway workshops of the Rajputana Malwa Railway in Ajmeer. This metre gauge line is an extension of the famous Bombay Baroda and Central India Railway. I always enjoyed my visits to this little Mission, its Sunday services, its confirmations, and the little social gatherings given in our welcome. At one time, many years ago, I suggested to the S.P.G. that it might be strengthened by a European missionary, but no one was available, and as things are I feel that one worthy Indian priest meets the needs of our Indian flock in Ajmeer.

CHAPTER IX

INDIAN PRINCES—ROYAL VISITORS

Indian Princes and their states—Chief colleges—The Princes' loyalty to the King Emperor—Royal visits to the native states in the Diocese—Their Royal Highnesses the Prince and Princess of Wales spend Christmas at Gwalior, 1905—The Crown Prince of Germany spends Christmas at Jaipur, Rajputana, 1910—The Prince of Wales visits Nagpur and Gwalior, 1922.

TWO-THIRDS of the Nagpur Diocese lies in the territories of about forty or more of our Indian Princes or Maharajahs, and so it is only to be expected that I have a good deal to say about them... There are in India a very large number of independent or semi-independent Indian rulers, some of whom are very wealthy and some quite the reverse. Those in the Diocese of Nagpur belong mostly to the rather wealthy and some very wealthy Indian rulers. When there was no supreme power in India there was fairly constant fighting between these Indian Princes, and at one time the territories of the historic chiefs of Rajputana would have largely passed into Mahratta rule had not the British prevented it. As the East India Company desired peace above all things largely for the sake of their trade, they gradually induced the majority of these princes to enter into treaty relations with them and their neighbours. By the year 1830 a large part of India had been " settled " and the East India Company had promised protection and independence under the British ægis and suzerainty to a very great number of these Indian Princes. Under these settlements some of the most successful fighters of those times, especially the Mahrattas, were assured of peaceful possession of the large territories they had won by the sword, and found themselves ruling over people who were of different race to themselves or even of different religion. For example, the Maharajah Scindhia of Gwalior is ruling over subjects comparatively few of whom are Mahrattas, and the Maharajah of Kashmir, himself a Hindu, rules over a country the vast majority of whose people are Mohammedan. In 1857, when a large section of the Indian Army was in rebellion, the Indian Princes remained loyal to the British Government, and since then their loyalty has steadily increased. If there is an element of self-interest in it as there well may be, they are sufficiently educated to realise the value of being linked up with a great Empire.

A very wise step was taken by the British Government when it established in various places colleges for the education of the sons of the Indian Princes and their nobility.   The first of these colleges was established at Rajkot in Kathiawar, in the north of the Bombay Presidency.   Its first Principal, Mr. Chester Macnaghten, was a man of great wisdom and ability. He understood very clearly what was needed in the training of these young Indian boys, and his lofty, Christian character and sincere goodness made a deep impression on his pupils. Among them was the famous cricketer, His Highness Ranjit-sinhji, the late Jam of Jamnagar.   Other colleges soon followed, the most famous being the Mayo College at Ajmeer, the Acheson College at Lahore, and the Daly College at Indore.   Smaller colleges were established in other parts of India, amongst them being the Rajkumar College at Raipari in the Central Provinces, whose former Principal is now Principal of the Mayo College at Ajmeer.

These Chiefs Colleges are run like English Public Schools. The boys being Hindus or Mohammedans, have every facility for practising their religion, Brahmin pandits being part of the recognised college staff.   The boys are all boarders, and each boy usually brings his own cook and two or three other servants.   A good many boys bring their ponies to college so that in a college of seventy boys there may be as many as two hundred ponies !   It need hardly be said that most of the boys are as much at home on a horse from early childhood as they are on their own feet. In these Chiefs Colleges each boy has his own sitting-room, bedroom and bathroom.   His servants are provided with quarters close to his rooms and the kitchen is hard by.   The playground of colleges, like the Mayo College at Ajmeer or the Daly College at Indore, is a very pretty sight with the boys in their white clothes and beautiful coloured turbans. The curriculum is arranged to give the boys a good knowledge of English, of their own vernacular, and a classical language such as Persian or Sauskrit. The subjects in the highest class in these colleges include the study of elementary law, land, revenue, surveying and other such subjects as may help the boys in their future life and work in their states. There are difficulties, as one of the Principals of a chief college described to me, sometimes with parents, sometimes about food and religious observances, sometimes with servants or the boys themselves, but these are forgotten in the satisfaction of seeing that a new type of educated chief is appearing in India and that old boys of the Chiefs Colleges are more careful for the welfare of their subjects than the old Rajahs of past histories. I should add that I have frequently been the guest of the Principals of these Chiefs Colleges, and shall always remember with pleasure the charming hospitality of Mr. and Mrs. Charles Waddington, Mr. and Mrs. Leslie Jones, and Mr. and Mrs. Percy Hide.

In the winter of 1908 I visited Nowgong in Central India. After spending a pleasant week-end with our soldiers, and visiting a Maharajah who wished to discuss religious questions, though I never felt he was a genuine seeker, I motored down to Panna about 100 miles to the south with Mr. W. E. Jardine, Political Agent of Bundelkhand, through a very pretty hilly country. Our visit was timed so as to bring us to Panna for the festivities connected with the fiftieth anniversary of the British Crown taking over the Government of India from the East India Company. Many of my readers will remember that after the mutiny in 1857 the East India Company's rule in India came to an end. By far the most striking piece of architecture in this remote Indian city is a huge Hindu temple dedicated to the God Vishnu and modelled on Christopher Wren's design for St. Paul's Cathedral in London. The architect of this temple, a Mr. Manley, a member of the domiciled European community, and head of the Public Works Department in Panna, informed me that, when ordered by the late Maharajah of Panna to build a large temple in the city, after much thought he decided to take the great Christian temple in London as his model! The fiftieth anniversary of the assumption of the supreme Government in India by the Crown was celebrated with great ceremony in Panna. Let me quote the official account of these ceremonies prepared by a state official under the Maharajah's orders. " A royal salute was fired in the morning, the army was paraded and a ' feu de joie' was fired. A holiday was observed in all the State offices and courts. Sweetmeats and puris were distributed to the hospital patients, orphanages and prisoners, and alms were given to about 500 beggars! The Sardar or State school boys were sumptuously fed. Games were held by the Sardar boys in the noon. In the temples and mosques prayers were offered by the Hindus and Mohammedans for the long life of His Majesty, King Edward VII., the Emperor, and the continuance of the British Raj. The town was decorated with triumphal arches bearing ' God save the Emperor' and ' Long live the Emperor.' The whole town, including temples, masjids, mosques, palace and other State buildings, was illuminated and a Jalsa was held at night attended by jagirdars, officials, gentries, pandits and mahants (abbots). The Jalsa proved a great success by the presence of a number of European officers and ladies including W. E. Jardine, Esq., I.C.S., Political Agent in Bundelkhand, the Right Rev. Dr. Chatterton, Lord Bishop of Nagpur, etc., etc. Prayers were offered for His Majesty the Emperor's ever enhancing health and prosperity by Pandits, Sardars, Hindi and vernacular school boys and munshis. In front of the Kothi (palace) fireworks were displayed. Musicians and akharewalas exhibited their performances. Gramophones were also played. Attar, pan, bouquets and garlands were distributed. The Jalsa was dissolved at about 11 o'clock in the night."

Shortly before proceedings in the courtyard of the Palace ended, the Pandit Kanhiya Lal Shastri, a Sanscrit teacher, recited the following verses, which are here translated into English : " My humble efforts fail to give vent to my feelings before this learned gathering, to whom I bow down, and apologise for all my shortcomings in expressing my joy in connection with the anniversary. But the encouragement and the generous disposition of the audience has emboldened me to utter a few words of rejoicings. Your Majesty's Empire so vast that the sun never sets on it. The proudest of Kings have been brought under subjugation and pay homage to you. May God protect Your Majesty for ever!

" Happy ever be the Emperor Edward VII., who rules over the whole Bharat Versha, and whose eulogies are sung by old and young of both the sexes. O, ye Shri Krishna Bhagwan, the destroyer of the Daitya Mur, evildoers, Daitya Buk, O God who with all the deities took incarnation in the lunar race, and whose resting place is in the ocean of the milk, may ever protect His Majesty the Emperor."

Another address composed for this occasion by the Pandit of Sardar Boarding House was also recited before us by the boys : " Happy is the day and blessed is the hour, the whole Panna gives vent to utterances in rejoicings for the Emperor Edward. Welcome to you great men and show us your brilliant faces and thereby confer happiness to us boys, and pour down your blessings on us. Come in the midst of this institution, you great men. Your enhancing prosperity is genuine pleasure to us boys. Living in this institution we come forward to give our respects to you and all those great men who are in your company. You, gentlemen, come in our midst and shower your blessings upon us. We boys feel happy on seeing your moonlike faces. O great men, please hear our humble prayers that we may ever enjoy the kindness of you all. Gokal Sharma pray that the Emperor may live long and rule over us for years to come. Come and take the seats in this humble institution. We know not in which way we can best honour you here and join us in offering prayers for Edward VII. who may live long and rule for ages."

I can recall several occasions in the Native States of my Diocese, where I witnessed the great efforts and even anxiety of the Indian Princes to show their loyalty to the King Emperor or his representative, the Viceroy of India. By far the most impressive scenes, however, that I can remember, took place at Gwalior in the winter of 1905 when their Royal

Highnesses, the Prince and Princess of Wales (our present King and Queen), spent a week there as guests of the Maharajah Scindhia. In the late summer of 1905 I was informed by the Metropolitan that their Royal Highnesses were coming to India and would spend several weeks in the Native States of my Diocese. I was told that I was to send chaplains to Udaipur in the State of Mewar, and to Bikanir on consecutive Sundays to conduct Divine Service. In addition to this I learnt that their Royal Highnesses would spend a week at Gwalior which included a Sunday and Christmas Day. For Gwalior I was asked to arrange for Sunday Services and was informed that their Royal Highnesses would receive the Holy Communion on Christmas Day.

Then came a decidedly disturbing piece of news, when the Rev. E. R. Clough, visiting chaplain of Gwalior, requested me to go to Gwalior as soon as possible as the roof of the little Church had been dismantled by the Chief Engineer, it being regarded as unsafe, and his congregation had to worship in the Club House. In former days there had been a period when the Mahrattas and the East India Company had been in open hostility, and for a fairly long period after hostilities had ceased, a large British force was maintained at Morar three miles from the Capital city of the State. Two Churches were built at that time by the military authorities for this garrison. Then when happier days dawned and the house of Scindhia became the friend of the British, the British garrison was removed to Jhansi in Central India, and the large garrison Church was dismantled. What had now happened was that just when it would be wanted the small Church of St. Peter's was roofless, and the small English congregation were holding their Sunday services in a large room in the social and amusements club. That the future King and Queen of England should have to attend their Christmas services in a roofless Church was inconceivable, and the idea of holding the services in a "Shamiana" or large tent, or in the Club House, in a place abounding in palaces and beautiful buildings, seemed impossible. I felt that the infant Diocese of Nagpur, poor though it was, must rise to the occasion, and that a roof must be on the Church

before Christmas, whatever it cost.   Mr. H. V. Cobb, then
Resident in Gwalior, fully agreed with me. With characteristic
generosity, His Highness, the late Maharajah, offered to meet
the cost, but while thanking him most cordially for his offer
we felt that either the Diocese or the Government of India
were the proper bodies to bear the cost.   As not a moment
could be lost if the roof was to be on the Church in time, I
asked two of the leading officials in Central India, the Honourable Major H. Daly and Mr. Cobb, to share with me the
responsibility of guaranteeing the amount in the event of
Government, to whom the Church belonged, declining to foot
the bill. Our guarantee was never required and with strenuous
efforts Mr. Lake, one of the State engineers, had the Church
ready some time before Christmas.

To fully appreciate all that took place during this visit of
their Royal Highnesses, one should read the really beautiful
book which, under the Maharajah's orders, was produced by
the late Mr. J. W. D. Johnstone, Director of Public Instruction
in the Gwalior State. Its beautiful illustrations and its accurate
description of the various State functions, the Royal entry, the
feudal ceremony in the Durbar Hall, the review, military
sports, the sham fight between the army of the Celestials and
Scindhia Army, the State Banquet, the tiger hunts and finally
our beautiful Sunday and Christmas services, are there given
with a wealth of detail.

No one who witnessed these scenes can ever forget them.
The whole setting of these functions was so splendid, the fine
Palaces and State buildings, and, above all, the great Fort of
Gwalior, towering above everything.   Let me picture very
briefly some of the events of thirty years ago which have left
the clearest memory in my mind.

First of all there was the State entry when, after
the Maharajah had introduced his leading nobles and the
leading British officials to their Royal Highnesses, the whole
party mounted thirty beautifully trained elephants covered
with grotesque designs.   One of the favourite designs which
was certainly most clever and original was that of a pair of
tigers one on each side of the elephant's trunk.   The eyes of

these tigers exactly coincided with those of the elephants so that when the elephant blinked his eyes, the tigers seemed to blink theirs. The Prince rode on the first elephant with the Maharajah under a magnificent howdah, and the Princess on the second elephant with the Honourable Major Hugh Daly, Agent to the Governor General for Central India. The magnificence of the procession was enhanced by the Mahratta Cavalry in costumes of former days. Early in the afternoon there took place in the Maharajah's Durbar Hall, or Hall of Assembly, a very striking feudal ceremony, when the Maharajah presented to the Prince his twelve leading nobles, who one and all presented their gifts or Nazars in the form of golden mohars to the Royal Representative of the King Emperor. The gifts were touched by the Prince according to custom and then returned. The Maharajah himself did likewise, presenting many beautiful things including five elephants which were duly received and returned. Later in the day the Prince and Princess drove to Lashkar, the native city, and opened a very fine new market place in memory of Queen Victoria. The streets were gay with all kinds of banners. One favourite piece of bunting across the street was " Tell Papa Gwalior subjects quite happy." At night the historic Fort of Gwalior, which rises like an island or some great promontory from the plains, with its frontage towards the city of over two miles, was one blaze of illuminations, and some thousands of fire balloons were let loose.

On the following day His Royal Highness reviewed the Maharajah's army of over 11,000 troops. The Artillery comprised six batteries of different kinds, two horse, one field, one heavy (elephant), and two bullock. There were three Lancer Regiments, reminiscent of the old Mahratta Light Cavalry, once the terror of the Moghul armies. The Maharajah, in the uniform of a British General, rode at the head of his Cavalry on a splendid grey horse. Was it by accident or design that a blue jay, that lovely bird emblem of peace, flew in front of the army? In the afternoon there were military sports with a most picturesque musical ride, the Mahratta Cavalry being in line forms of pre-hunting days. Later on there was a most realistic sham fight with the taking of a fort occupied by a Chinese General Fi Tang and his Chinese force. There was the usual exchange of artillery, counter charges of cavalry, and when the Celestials were finally defeated, the Red Cross doolie or stretcher-bearers carried off the slain and wounded.

Then came the State banquet, in the very fine Banqueting Hall, when one hundred and thirty guests sat down to dinner. The Royal Table was beautifully decorated in white and silver with a profusion of flowers and ferns. The Hall was admirably lit, as in addition to electric lights suspended from the ceiling, dainty little shaded lamps were placed along the tables. The device for passing wine and cigarettes and sweets round the Royal Table was both novel and extremely pretty. A miniature silver electric train with a silver engine and six cut glass coaches running on rails (the Scindhia Light Railway) was set in motion by a switch fixed by the Prince's side by which he could start, accelerate, or stop the train at his pleasure; and I can well recall the immense amusement caused by the advantage which His Royal Highness took of his place and power over the train when some outstretched hands found the train either stop just out of reach, or move too swiftly past them. Then came the toasts and a fine loyal speech by the Maharajah to which His Royal Highness gave a most striking reply. Passing over the tiger shoots to which only a few of the Maharajah's guests were invited, and where the Prince, who is a fine shot, killed three tigers, I come to Christmas and the Christmas services. In arranging for them I can well remember how much help we got from the late Sir Arthur Bigge, afterwards Lord Stamfordham.

First came Sunday, which fell on Christmas Eve, and Christmas Day, which I think everyone welcomed as a rest from these succession of ceremonies. Their Royal Highnesses and their staff attended services on both days and I had the responsibility of being the special preacher on both occasions. Our services were made additionally attractive as we had the band of the Prince's own regiment, the 10th Royal Hussars, and a dozen fine male voices from the choir of Mhow Church.

Our efforts had been completely successful as far as the Church was concerned, and St. Peter's, Morar, built of local stone with its rather massive stone tower looked just like a pretty little village Church in old England. There was, however, one difference; it had been impossible to grow a nice grass lawn around it at such short notice, but few, if any, save Mr. Lake and myself and one or two others, knew that the green sward they saw was nothing but young wheat sown thickly, and a couple of inches above the ground! The Christmas hymns were sung beautifully. Their Royal Highnesses made their Communion, and the collection on Christmas Day was for our Cathedral Building Fund in Nagpur, the first that was ever made for that object, and amounted to nearly £50.

On Christmas Eve I had the honour of dining with the Prince and Princess at the Jai Bilas Palace, where they and their immediate staff were staying. After dinner the late Maharajah, Sir Pertap Singh, a famous old Rajput and great sportsman, came up to me and in his amusing English asked, "Why you stop Prince shoot Sunday?" When I replied that I had not done so, but that on Sunday His Royal Highness felt it his duty to go to Church and worship God, and keep the day quietly, he still persisted in his assertion and finished up by saying, "Prince go to Church. Tiger kill deer. Why you stop Prince shoot Sunday?" Needless to say we were both of us laughing heartily before our talk ended. He was a great old man was the Maharajah, polite and courteous, and I cannot refrain from telling one story about him told me by the late Sir John Milbanke, which occurred about this time. The Maharajah had invited a party of the Prince's staff to do some pig-sticking in his State of Idar. The late Sir John Milbanke, then in the 10th Hussars, was among them. When galloping after a pig, Sir John's horse, a beautiful animal belonging to the Maharajah, put his foot in a hole and came down with a broken leg, and had to be shot. Fortunately, Sir John escaped without anything worse than a rather severe shaking. When he went to the Maharajah full of regrets at the accident, the Maharajah put him at his ease in the following way: "My horse break his leg, you not worry. You break your neck, I not worry."

On Christmas afternoon there was a Christmas tree provided by the Maharajah to which about forty children were invited, five of them English, and thirty-five Indian, the sons and daughters of Gwalior officials. The Prince and Princess gave away the presents. The Father Christmas on this occasion was Sir Michael Filose, a Knight of the Holy Roman Empire and one of the leading officials in the State.

Thus ended a most historic and delightful week in which the Maharajah had given all his numerous guests every conceivable kind of amusement and happiness, including a charming Christmas box on our dressing tables on Christmas Day. In the years which followed I had opportunities of seeing and knowing more and more of this most attractive and kindly Indian Prince which I shall refer to later on. Before saying a final good-bye to that famous Christmas camp at Gwalior, and before the sea of splendid tents was broken up, and the leading journalists from England and India had passed on with the Royal party to their next halt on the Royal tour, I must speak of one of the sights in Gwalior which filled most of the guests with a good deal of wonder.

In olden days the lion found a home in Central India, just as well as the tiger. The last lion in Central India had been shot about seventy years before. When Sir Thomas Roe, our first Ambassador from the Court of King James I. to the Moghul Court at Delhi, visited Mandhu, not fifty miles from Mhow, he speaks of lions carrying off their dogs. The Maharajah Scindhia conceived the idea of bringing back these animals to his State, and Lord Kitchener presented him with two magnificent African lions and their mates. They were kept in a large enclosure with immensely high walls and were fed on live quarry. One could hear their mighty roars as one lay peacefully in one's bed. Everyone went to see them and the story was current that when the Prince saw a large Roman-nosed Indian goat standing up to one of the lions unafraid, he said its life must be saved. This was done and the Prince presented it with a silver collar on which was inscribed Daniel! But the story goes further. In due course the lions were let loose and then the trouble began. Instead of behaving like nice lions, and attacking deer and old bullocks, they began to attack the villagers with such serious results that it was decided they must be recaptured and put back in the enclosure. But the lions were enjoying their freedom, and were not at all ready to go back to their prison. Eventually a Eurasian official, Mr. Onraet, devised a decidedly novel method of capturing them. In a large hut where a " kill " was to be tied up the floors and walls were covered over with stickfast fly paper. When the lions entered the hut to get their victims the paper stuck on their paws and bodies, and in scratching themselves the paper got into their eyes and so they were soon got into cages and taken back into captivity. What their future has been I cannot tell.

Five years later my wife and I received an invitation from His Highness the Maharajah of Jaipur, Rajputana, to be his guests when he was entertaining His Royal Highness the late Crown Prince of Germany at Christmas. As I was informed that, in addition to the Crown Prince's fairly large German and British staff, there would be a number of leading English officials and other friends of the Maharajah's, and as there was no chaplain available to conduct the Christmas services, I felt it was clearly my duty to accept the Maharajah's kind invitation, even though it meant a thirty-six hours railway journey. The Maharajah and some of his leading Rajput nobles, together with Sir Elliot Colvin, the Agent to the Governor General, Colonel Showers, the Resident of Jaipur, Sir Swinton Jacob, and a few more of the guests met His Royal Highness on his arrival. After the usual introductions the Crown Prince and the Maharajah drove off to the old Palace in the Maharajah's State carriage under a Royal umbrella. The special feature of the escort was a large company of Meenas, an aboriginal race, highly esteemed in the State, who ran in front, at the side, and behind the royal carriage with their native weapons. These Meenas are the guardians of the forts and other important buildings in Jaipur. As the Maharajah's principal guests were entertained at the same Palace as the Crown Prince and his staff, we had the honour of dining daily with the Royal visitor. He was clearly out to enjoy himself, and to make all who were near him enjoy themselves. On the first night at dinner after the ladies had withdrawn, he beckoned to me without the formality of sending one of his staff, to come over and speak to him. He was obviously very fond of sport and games. He told me that he was specially fond of lawn tennis, and that the professional who played with him a great deal was one George Carr, who had been our professional at the Fitzwilliam Club in Dublin in my University days, and with whom I had played a good deal. He also told me how much he approved of our young English clergy playing games with their people, adding in a most humorous way that, as for the German clergy, neither of their two feet were on earth!

Everything had been carefully arranged as to his entertainment during the three or four days he stayed at Jaipur. There was the usual pig-sticking and tiger shooting. What might have been a very serious, if not fatal, accident to the Crown Prince when riding after a boar, was averted by the fine horsemanship of my friend, Mr. C. E. Stotherd, State Engineer, who seeing that the pig was heading for a dangerous ravine or nullah, and that the Prince was unaware of his danger, galloped in between the Prince and the nullah and stuck the pig.

On Christmas Eve General Count von Dohnu of the Prussian Guards, the senior military member of the staff, asked permission of Lady Colvin, who with Mrs. Showers the Resident's wife, were acting hostesses on behalf of the Maharajah, if they might sing their Christmas carols. The whole of the staff, including the valets, took part in this carol singing, the Crown Prince himself playing extremely well on the violin, and the doctor from German East Africa playing on the piano. They sang some of their beautiful German carols with deep feeling. When they had finished, Dr. Wegener, the historian of the party, turned to me with the query, "You have no carols in England?" Fortunately, before leaving Nagpur, I had brought some of the music of

Dr. Stainer's carols and a couple of dozen copies of the words, and we had among the English guests a number of persons who knew the carols and could sing extremely well. The carol of ours which the Crown Prince's party most fancied was " Good King Wenceslas."

When Christmas Day arrived the Crown Prince expressed a wish to come to Church. Though we have no resident chaplain at Jaipur, we have a very beautiful little English Church which had been built by the late Sir Swinton Jacob. His name will be remembered in Rajputana for many a long day as many of its most beautiful buildings and some of the Palaces of its Maharajahs were designed and built by him. The Christmas lessons were read at my invitation by the Rev. Dr. George Macalister, a splendid old Presbyterian missionary who had spent forty years in missionary work in Jaipur. He was a blood brother of the Meenas who were custodians of Amber, the old and deserted capital of the State. Our organist was the bandmaster of the Maharajah's band.

In my sermon, it being Christmas Day, I dwelt very naturally on what the world owed to our Lord Jesus Christ, and I quoted the saying attributed to Napoleon on the island of St. Helena, referred to in Canon Liddon's famous lectures on the Divinity of our Lord : " Jesus Christ was more than man. . . I have inspired multitudes with such an enthusiastic devotion that they would have died for me . . . but to do this it was necessary that I should be visibly present with the electric influence of my looks, of my words, of my voice. When I saw men and spoke to them, I lighted up the flame of self-devotion in their hearts. . . . Christ alone has succeeded in so raising the mind of man toward the Unseen that it becomes insensible to the barriers of time and space. Across a chasm of eighteen hundred years, Jesus Christ makes a demand which is above all others difficult to satisfy. He asks for the human heart. He will have it entirely to Himself. He demands it unconditionally, and forthwith His demand is granted. Wonderful! In defiance of time and space, the soul of man, with all its powers and faculties, becomes an annexation to the Empire of Christ." Before dinner the Crown Prince came up to me

I

and asked where I had found this statement as he thought he had read every book about Napoleon.

There was, of course, a State Banquet given by the Maharajah at his Palace, and the Pink City was brilliantly illuminated. One of the German staff rather wittily remarked, " It's worth being a Maharajah when you can order the whole of your city to be painted pink." I own I had almost forgotten the Crown Prince's remark that he wished to play me a match at lawn tennis, when on the afternoon before he left I was informed that he was waiting for me on the tennis courts. In my University days I had played in a good many tournaments, and had been fortunate enough to beat the American champion in the finals of the Midland Counties Championship of England at Buxton in 1885, but it certainly was a novel experience to play this match with all the Prince's staff, German and English, looking on. I felt sure that the Prince was far too good a sportsman not to wish me to really play up, but when the late Sir H. Stuart, the leading English official on the Prince's staff, whispered in my ear as I left the court : " Bishop, you are no courtier," I felt a little twinge of doubt, which was, however, soon dispelled when the Prince himself said that he would like me to come to Potsdam and play him another match on his own courts.

Once more in the winter of 1922 the Diocese of Nagpur was visited by Royalty, when His Royal Highness the Prince of Wales visited Nagpur and Gwalior. I was unfortunately attending the Synod of Bishops in Calcutta when he visited Nagpur, but I had the honour and good fortune of being once more the guest of the Maharajah Scindhia when he visited Gwalior. Some time before he visited Nagpur a local Indian poet who loved to chant the praises of kings and great men, came to see me about a poem which he had composed in honour of the Prince. He wanted me to let him know whether I thought the Prince would approve of it. When I suggested that the words " the would-be king " should be altered to " the future king," I was told by my household critic that I was cutting out the only really amusing bit of the poet's efforts.

The Prince's visit to Gwalior brought back to my memory all the stirring scenes of his father's, our King's, visit in 1905. It was, of course, quite a short visit with none of the many ceremonies and functions of the former one. Doubtless there were the same number of tigers shot, and the same, if not greater, desire on the part of the Maharajah to do honour to the son of our Sovereign for whom he entertained something more than loyalty, a real personal affection. At our Sunday morning service, quite a short one with a three minutes sermon, the Maharajah himself attended with the Prince, and again about £50 was given in the collection for my Anglo-Indian Children's Home at Nagpur, the Maharajah himself contributing Rs. 500.

Another of the many visits I paid to Gwalior was a peculiarly pleasant one, as while I was staying with the Resident, Mr. W. E. Jardine, we were invited to a picnic by the Maharajah in a jungle near his hot weather residence. We were the only European guests, and it was good to see the Maharajah treating the General of his army and his other officials in the most delightful and brotherly way, and to note their high regard for him not only as their Prince but as a man.

There was an American Mission in Gwalior, and when an old American missionary lady, who had worked there for years, died, so great was His Highness's respect for her that he and his life-long friend, Colonel Crofts, helped to carry her coffin from the house to the carriage which bore it to her grave. When I paid my last visit to Gwalior after his death, the place seemed to me so changed without its kindly master that I was almost glad to think I would not see it again.

CHAPTER X

A Chaplain's work—The Anglo-Indian Community—The building of Churches.

WHEN I first went to India in 1892 as a missionary, the Bishop of Chota Nagpur asked me to act as Chaplain to the English and Anglo-Indian people in Hazaribagh station and district. This involved visits every two months to the East Indian Railway Collieries at Giridih, as well as to a number of young Englishmen who were engaged in mica mining in the north of the district. At Giridih there was a fairly large European Community, with a certain number of men from the collieries in the Midlands. I greatly valued this opportunity of trying to help spiritually my fellow countrymen, many of whom were living far away from the land of their birth, exposed to many temptations and surrounded by a large non-Christian population. I think it is a great help to a missionary who is spending most of his days in trying to convince Hindus and Moslems of the truth of Christianity, to break off for short periods and minister to Christian people. Almost at once I realised what a great variety there is amongst the domiciled European and Anglo-Indian people in India, some of pure British descent connected with India for several generations, some of mixed descent whose remote British ancestor came out in the service of the East India Company.

One day within a few months of our arrival in India, when the hot weather had set in, I received an urgent request from an Anglo-Indian lady, the widow of a Crimean veteran, to accompany her on a visit to a local petty Rajah. Her son who was in this Rajah's employ as a groom was getting into bad company, and the mother was most anxious to get him away and at the same time to persuade the Rajah to give him several months of back pay. We had to drive nearly sixteen miles in a small dog-cart, and as it was very hot we started

at daylight. On arrival we were informed that the Rajah
would see us later on, and as we were offered no shelter in
his palace, and there was no Dak bungalow anywhere near,
we picnicked under the shade of a grove of mango trees.
Fortunately we had brought with us food and water.
Frequently during the day messages passed from us to the
Rajah asking when he could see us, and as frequently the
reply came that he would see us later on. When evening set
in, and I saw that the Rajah had no intention of giving us an
interview, I told the widow's son that with or without his
back pay he must come with us and leave the Rajah's service.
When a few days later I happened to meet a member of my
congregation, a Scottish tea-planter, who acted in some way
as an agent for the Rajah, I mentioned the matter to him
rather casually. I had no intention of making any fuss about
what was unquestionably a great act of rudeness on the part
of this petty Rajah. My friend, however, treated the matter
very differently. He at once went to the Rajah and asked
him if he at all realised what he had done ! Did he know that
the Rev. Eyre Chatterton was a friend of Queen Victoria, and
that she had come down to Tilbury to say good-bye to him
when he was leaving for India ! Then a few days later the
Rajah sent me a present of a seventeen hand Australian
" Waler " horse, which I at once returned, causing dismay
amongst his staff. Then later on the Rajah himself came to
offer his apologies. Whether the young man ever got his back
pay, leaving as he did, I cannot say, but the memory of how
I tried to help the Anglo-Indian lady has never been forgotten, nor its rather amusing termination.

When I found myself in charge of the new Diocese of
Nagpur, and began my long series of tours and explorations,
I soon learnt that there were a very large number of persons
of this kind for whose spiritual welfare our Church was
responsible. Three or four things were, I saw, imperatively
necessary. We must find out where they were, what they were
doing, and what they needed. They must be visited by our
chaplains regularly, and given all the spiritual help which the
Church had in its power to give them. If the community was

not too small and they had no place in which to worship, a Church must be provided. If they had children we must do all in our power to have them educated. There were at least sixty of such communities, some large, some small, dotted over these Central regions of India. Many of the men were employed in the railways (it is said that 7,000 retired British soldiers are on the Indian railways!), some in collieries, and some in manganese mines. There were four coalfields in different parts of the Central Provinces, and a number of manganese mines. These small out-stations, as we call them in India, are visited periodically by our clergy. Everyone in India knows that our chaplains, in addition to work in their headquarters' station, may have as many as half a dozen out-stations to visit, some of them being one or two hundred miles from where they live.

As regards places of worship, for our own people, that is often a real problem. The need is there but the money to build is very scarce. When Sir Richard Temple, the first Chief Commissioner of the Central Provinces, was appointed, he made enquiries as to how the European officials and their subordinates were provided with places of worship in their headquarter stations. The result was, as I found in 1903, a fair number of the civil-stations with quite nice little stone Churches. In some places they had even converted buildings no longer used for the purpose for which they had been built into quite useful, if rather quaint Churches. A disused powder magazine had been made into quite a nice little Church at Betul, and in two places, Damoh and Narsinghpur, disused magistrates' courts had been converted into Churches. The places where Churches were most urgently needed were, as I soon saw, for railway communities dotted along the hundreds of miles of our Indian railway systems. Running through the Diocese of Nagpur were the Great Indian Peninsula, the Bengal Nagpur, the Bombay Baroda and Central India, and the Rajputana Malwa Railways.

Let me explain our method of procedure in facing the problem of Church building for these communities. Having summoned a meeting of the people concerned and having learnt whether they were really anxious to have a Church of their own, it was decided to open a subscription list in the place itself. In most of these smallish railway communities there might be one or two railway officials, but no more. The other men of importance in the community were the station master, engine drivers, guards, a permanent way inspector, and ticket collectors. Sometimes it took years before the amount needed could reach such a figure as to justify us in appealing for outside help. This help, when sought, must come, so we knew, from three sources, each of which had to be assured that the people for whom the Church was needed had done all in their power to contribute towards it. The first source of outside help would naturally be the Diocesan Board of Finance. The second would be the railway company for whose employees the Church was needed, and the third would be our much loved and valued S.P.C.K. S.P.C.K. never failed us, and how the church overseas would get on without S.P.C.K. I cannot imagine. These little Churches were not costly buildings, five or six hundred pounds in India, where labour and material are cheap, gave us quite a nice little Church.

There are quite interesting little bits of history connected with the building of some of these Railway Churches. When I first visited Bhopal, the capital of the chief Mohammedan state in Central India, I held my first confirmation in the waiting room of the Railway station. I remember how the Indian servants from the refreshment room kept peeping in to see what the " Lat Padre " Sahib was doing. To fully appreciate what one must regard as the humiliation of a Christian community of English and Anglo-Indians having no better place to worship in, one must remember that Bhopal had a number of magnificent mosques and not a few Hindu temples. It took nineteen years to raise the money needed for the building of the little railway Church of The Redeemer at Bhopal, and I felt most happy at being able to consecrate it before I left India in 1926. I knew, too, the very deep joy that filled the hearts of our people in Bhopal that they now had a Church of their own.

Another small Church in the native state of Rutlam in Central India was consecrated by me a few years after the War. When I laid its foundation stone a silver trowel was presented to me with the following inscription : " This trowel was used by the Right Rev. The Lord Bishop of Nagpur for laying the foundation of the Church of England in Rutlam " ! I shall never forget the number of presents which poured in on the occasion of the consecration of this Church of St. Bartholomew, Rutlam, as an evidence of the pride and joy they felt in their own little place of worship in this Hindu State.

At Khandwa in the Central Provinces we had the extraordinary problem of having two Churches, neither of which was the least suitable. The first of the Churches, St. Andrew's, was built when a Madras regiment with British officers was stationed there. It was nearly two miles from the place where the railway people lived, and I never once held a service in it. The other Church, St. Catherine's, was in the railway station yard, within sixty yards of the railway lines, noisy and dirty. This Church of St. Catherine, which had been used for a school as well as a Church, was built by Dr. Peter Cullen and his friend, Father O'Neill of the Society of St. John Baptist, Cowley, Oxford.

Father O'Neill as a young man had been a mathematical master at Eton. After ordination he had worked under the famous Canon Carter, Warden of Clewer, for a time, and had then joined the Cowley Fathers. When he was sent to their Mission in India, after a period in Bombay and Poona, he moved to Indore, a Mahratta city in Central India. Here he lived, in the bazaar, a life of intense simplicity and self-denial. He gathered round him a body of young Christian converts who shared in his life of devotion. One of these, Samuel Gopal, was afterwards Verger of our Church in Mhow. His devotion during one of the plague epidemics filled the Hindus and Moslems with deep awe and veneration. On Sundays he would sometimes preach in the little English Church to the great delight and edification of the European community, which included the Agent to the Governor-

General for Central India, the Resident of Indore, and other British officials. During his visits to Khandwa he made the acquaintance of Dr. Cullen, then Civil Surgeon, and together they planned and raised the money to build St. Catherine's Church. For eight years Father O'Neill lived and laboured in Indore. There he died and there he is buried. One of his greatest English friends in Indore was Aberich Mackay, the Principal of the Holker College, and author of that famous book " Twenty-one Days in India " in which he gives the most inimitable sketches bordering on caricatures of leading English officials in India. It always seemed to me a strangely happy, if pathetic sight, to see the graves of Aberich Mackay and Father O'Neill, side by side, in our Indore cemetery, the brilliant wit and this wholly consecrated man of God in death undivided.

Father O'Neill left a very deep impression on all who met him, and it was, I doubt not, his influence which led Dr. Cullen, after he retired from Government service, to be ordained. He settled in Jubbulpore where he and his wife are buried, and spent all his latter days in helping our poor Anglo-Indians, spiritually, medically and financially. Largely at his own expense he built and later on restored a little railway Church at Sohagpur, dedicated to St. Peter, and I can recall some very happy visits to that little station when I was entertained by a most excellent couple, Mr. Gracie, a permanent way inspector and his kindly wife.

But to return to Khandwa and its two Churches. When I found that neither of them was the least suitable for the railway community, and that a most unhappy incident prevented our making any financial appeal in the place itself, I approached the then Chief Commissioner, Sir Benjamin Robertson, with a request that he forward to the G.I.P. Railway a proposal, viz. that we should hand over to the railway companies the valuable land close to their railway station on which St. Catherine's Church stood, and that in return their engineers should dismantle both Churches and rebuild St. Andrew's on a site near their railway bungalows. After some discussion the directors of the

G.I.P. Railway and the Rajputana Malwa Railway, both of whom were interested in the station, agreed to the suggestion. Both Churches were then dismantled, and a very nice stone Church now stands in a position which suits everyone. As this Church was taking the place of St. Andrew's and St. Catherine's, we decided to give it a double dedication : the Church of St. Andrew's with St. Catherine's. Some memorial tablets were removed from St. Catherine's including one to Father O'Neill.

We were also able to build Churches for the railway people at Bilaspore, Dongargarh, Badnera, and Sambalpur, and to start funds for building Churches at Nainpur, Angani, Gangapur City and Itarsi. At Itarsi the G.I.P. Railway gave us a railway carriage, tiled over and raised on wooden piles as a temporary Church.

As I have already indicated, the care of the domiciled European and Anglo-Indian communities had been very much in my mind from my earliest days in India. I realised more and more what a definite responsibility they were to England, and especially to the Church of England. I got to know from books like Stark's " Hostages to India " the great services which their ancestors, the descendants of the pioneer Englishmen, had rendered in building up British rule and trade and prestige in India. I learnt how badly their services had been rewarded and how English people in India, knowing nothing of their past history and services, instead of sympathising and helping them, too often despised them and spoke most untruly of them. When I look back on my work in India, nothing gives me more pleasure than to think I had some share in providing a Home near our Cathedral in Nagpur for fifty of the very poor children of this Community. Started by Canon and Mrs. G. D. Philip in their Mission House at Takli, and carried on by them for over ten years, it was for another ten years carried on in its new and handsome building by the Cathedral, by an extremely capable and devoted Scottish lady, Miss Eleanor Renny-Tailyour. This was a bit of work well worth doing, " Inasmuch as ye have done it unto the least of these my little ones, ye have done it unto me."

One feature of the Anglo-Indian Community deserves some attention and commendation, viz. the readiness to help one another when in trouble. Letters have recently come to me from India telling how poor families, whose bread-winners are out of employment, have been helped by others in a remarkable way. One instance of the thoughtfulness of the better off Anglo-Indian for the poorer members of their own community occurred during my last days in India. A man called Stephen Joseph, who had been for many years a covenanted engine driver on the G.I.P. Railway and who had been married for many years to an Anglo-Indian lady, confirmed by me in 1904, was unfortunate enough to lose her in a plague epidemic in 1923. Before her death they had often spoken together about how they could dispose of their property. He had been of the saving type, and had a fine bungalow and a large Cinema. They had no near relations, and before his death a year later, he had willed all his property, which was valued at about £7,000, to be held in trust by the Anglican and Roman Catholic Bishops of Nagpur for the benefit of the poor European and Anglo-Indian community of Jubbulpore and neighbourhood. Part of the property consisted of a fine Cinema, and under the terms of the will it was not to be sold. It was an amusing position to be placed in, but as Monsignor Coppel, the Roman Catholic Bishop, and I were very friendly, we had no difficulty in settling everything satisfactorily. One of the Cinema proprietors in Nagpur, a Mr. Kale, arranged with us to carry it on, and as it was in Cantonments I knew that the General would never allow anything objectionable or derogatory to our race and especially to white women. We used the £150 a year which we each got as our share from it for helping our poorer children with scholarships. We placed over the grave of Stephen Joseph and his wife a headstone with the text: " Blessed is he that considereth the poor and needy, the Lord will deliver him in the time of trouble."

My wife and I had a sincere regard for Bishop Coppel. He and his French priests belonged to the Order of St. Francis de Sales. In 1930, when visiting

Annecy in Haute Savoie, I sent him a picture post card of his native city to Nagpur with our best wishes. Three months later I had a letter from him from Devizes in Wiltshire. He was on a short visit to Europe to report to His Holiness the Pope about his work, and was visiting Devizes where he had served as a Curate for two years before going to India. My wife and I asked him to pay us a visit before returning to India but as this was impossible, he lunched with us at the East India Club, where he met several of our retired English officials whom he had known in India. Six months later he passed onward into fuller light.

One of his priests, Father Montaignoux, was a friend of mine, and was much liked by the English officials in the Central Provinces. He was for many years the Roman Catholic Chaplain of Pachmarhi. He took a great interest in the English Church, knew the names of all the English Bishops, and could even tell you who was to be the next Archbishop of Canterbury! One good story is told of him. A certain Colonel in Pachmarhi, an English Baronet, was married to the daughter of a Colonial Governor. She had told her friends that she was a good deal younger than she really was. One day she met Father Montaignoux who had been reading Burke's peerage and had seen that she was born in a given year. When he said to her, " Oh, Lady C——, I see you are the daughter of ——, and were born in ——," her only remark was, " Dear Father Montaignoux, don't tell Mrs. —— " ! I went to see the dear old man shortly before his death to say good-bye. I remember his saying in his kind old way, " You know, Bishop, I shall never change your views, and you will never change mine."

PART II
1914—26

THE WAR AND AFTER

CHAPTER XI

THE WAR. 1914—18

Our Military Stations—The Central India Horse—Our Government
Chaplains—Their Work—The Great War—Our Clergy in various War
areas.

OUR military stations in India are placed with two considera-
tions in view, the maintenance of peace within our borders,
and the defence of our widespread frontiers. In the early days
of our struggles with the French and with some of the native
princes in South India, we were compelled to concentrate
large bodies of troops in those regions. To-day our cantonments at Bangalore and Secunderabad remind us of those
thrilling days. Our military status in the Central Provinces
and Central India, Jubbulpore, Kamptee, Saugor, Nowgong,
Mhow and Neemuch all link themselves with the wars with
the Mahrattas, more than a century ago. Then in still later
days came our wars with the Sikhs in the Punjab, and fightings
on the North-West Frontier and with the Afghans, which led
to the big concentration of troops at Rawal Pindi, Peshawar,
and along that frontier. As the Pax Britannica has spread
all over the country, the necessity of maintaining large bodies
of troops in Southern and Central India has considerably
diminished. When Lord Kitchener, fresh from his experiences
in South Africa, became Commander in Chief, his policy was
to strengthen our army in northern India in view of the pos-
sibility of trouble with Afghanistan and Russia, and to bring
smaller garrisons into our larger cantonments, so that the
training of the men for war should be thoroughly efficient.
For this reason three of the military stations in the Nagpur
Diocese, Nowgong, Neemuch and Saugor, which were in full
swing in 1903 when I first came to the Diocese, have practically ceased to have any military value, though Saugor still has
the Cavalry School for India. Of our four remaining cantonments, Mhow and Jubbulpore are the largest. Mhow, sometimes described, owing to its excellent climate, as a third-class

hill station, is about sixteen miles from Indore in plateau country. It had, during my episcopate, a Divisional Headquarters, and for many years before the Great War had a British Cavalry Regiment, two battalions of Royal Horse Artillery, a British Infantry and two Indian Infantry Regiments. Jubbulpore had its two British Infantry Regiments, one or two Indian Infantry Regiments, two battalions of Royal Field Artillery, and for a time, an Indian Cavalry Regiment. During Lord Kitchener's period of command in India, a gun carriage factory for all India was placed in Jubbulpore. The cantonment at Kamptee, with its British Infantry, one Battery of Field Artillery and an Indian Infantry Regiment, was guarding our lives and interests, being but ten miles from Government Headquarters in the big Mahratta city of Nagpur; and Nasirabad our sole British cantonment in Rajputana with a Brigadier and his brigade was on the edge of the British enclosure of Ajmeer.

I have already spoken of the Bhil Corps in Rajputana and Central India, raised originally by Sir James Outram to suppress dacoity, but my story would be quite incomplete without telling of the two small military stations of Agar and Goonah where for over fifty years two of our most famous Indian Cavalry Regiments were stationed. The history of the Central India Horse goes back to Mutiny days. In the days before the Mutiny some of the native rulers in Central India maintained contingents of Indian troops led by British officers. When the Mutiny broke out and death and destruction were widespread, three British officers, Mayne, Meade and Beatson, raised regiments of cavalry among those who had remained loyal to the British; and after many deeds of valour, captured the Nana's brilliant and cruel leader, Tantia Topi, who was duly executed. Mayne, who was a brilliant and daring cavalry soldier, was eventually given command of these cavalry regiments which for a time were called Mayne's Horse. Later on when he retired they received their well known name, the Central India Horse. Still later the regiments were further honoured by the appointment of His Royal Highness the Prince of Wales as its Colonel-in-Chief, and by the title, The

Prince of Wales' Own. One of the regiments was quartered at Agar, and the other at Goonah, both in the State of Gwalior to the south. To command one of the regiments of Central India Horse became the coveted prize for distinguished officers of Bengal Cavalry.

Here let me quote from a distinguished cavalry general who wrote in our Nagpur Diocesan Magazine on this famous regiment : " Men whose gallant deeds at Delhi and Lucknow had made their names conspicuous throughout the Empire were in return rewarded with the command of the Central India Horse, Henry Daly, Crawford, Chamberlain, Hughes, Deighton Probyn, John Watson, succeeded one another and left behind them a legacy of an honourable name. The conditions of life in such a regiment attracted the best type of officer in the British Army, the sportsman. Men like Martin, Neill and Gerard, for whom sport and soldiering were the only two objects in life, who slew their tigers by the hundred, have helped to make the traditions of the regiment what they are. For there are no society functions at Agar and Goonah. He who would join the Central India Horse must be prepared to rely for his amusements upon sport and polo alone. It must not be supposed that life at Agar and Goonah is one of pleasure alone. There is strenuous work to do, for the conditions of modern warfare demand from the military man a very high standard of efficiency and no regiment that is not thoroughly up-to-date in all its duties can aspire to the soldier's highest ambition to be sent on active service."

I have a few very pleasant memories connected with visits to Agar and Goonah. At Agar, conspicuous on the highest point of ridge, stood a very pretty little Church built by Colonel Martin. It was consecrated by Bishop Johnson in 1882, and was known popularly as St. Martin-in-the-Fields ! One morning after the Communion Service, shortly before I was leaving, Colonel Watson invited me to join the regiment in one of their favourite pastimes, a panther shoot. Mounting me on one of his beautiful and favourite polo ponies, a perfect mount, we started away for the bit of country where it was believed the panther was lying up. Our beaters were the

K

Sowars armed with spears. Unfortunately, the day was a blank, but none the less it was a pleasant experience to be with them and take part in this bit of innocent sport.

Since those days great changes have taken place. Under the concentration policy, begun by Lord Kitchener, Agar and Goonah have both been closed down and the memorials which covered the walls of the little Church have been transferred to our central Church of St. Anne's at Indore. " Sic transit gloria mundi." I shall always remember with gratitude the kindness I received from the C.I.H. and especially from Colonel Watson for letting me have Cinderella, my wife's beautiful mare. She was called Cinderella by her because she came from Central India !

The spiritual care of our British soldiers in India is in the hands of clergy appointed by the Secretary of State for India, and not by the War Office. They are usually called Government Chaplains. There is no service in British India so old as the Chaplains' service. It goes back over three centuries to the earliest days of the British in India. The London Company of Merchants which received its charter at the end of the reign of Queen Elizabeth, sent chaplains from England to their principal factories. When collecting materials for my " History of the Church of England in India since the days of the East India Company," I soon realised the important part which these chaplains of ours have taken during the last three centuries and the number of really able and devoted men who have served the Church in India. In the East India Company's days, their Chaplains ministered to military and civilian alike, and when after the Indian Mutiny the Crown took over the rule in India, the Indian Government carried on the same policy as far as the Chaplains' Department was concerned. Now things are changing. When, after the Great War, the Inchcape Commission visited India for the purpose of scrutinising and cutting down expenditure where possible, the Chaplains' Department was not overlooked. Before the Great War the number of Government Chaplains on the Ecclesiastical Establishment was 167, which was speedily reduced to 129. Since then further reductions have taken

CINDERELLA AND PADDY

place and I understand that the number to-day is rather less than 120. It seems practically certain that before many years the only Government Chaplains in India will be those maintained for our British soldiers. Meanwhile, the Government of India, realising the difficulties in which this inevitable change of policy has affected the Church, is making grants-in-aid to certain of the Bishops to assist them in paying for Diocesan Chaplains. How long that assistance may be given in the rapidly changing conditions in India no one can say.

In times past I personally got much help from our missionaries in what was called " out-station " work. They readily visited small places where scattered groups of English and Anglo-Indian people lived, and I feel convinced that in coming days we shall have to look to our missionary clergy to take a much larger part in ministering to their fellow-countrymen and Anglo-Indians in areas where their missions are working. This will be in many ways an excellent thing. It will bring both sides of the Church's work, the pastoral work for our own countrymen, and the evangelistic work amongst non-Christians closer together, and may inspire many of the Anglo-Indian Community to become actively missionary-minded. I need only repeat what I have often said about my earliest days in India, how I found it a great relief to switch off for a few days from trying to convince Hindus and Mohammedans of the truth of our Faith to the familiar task of an English parish priest.

The question has been raised from time to time as to the advisability of placing our Indian military stations under the care of chaplains from the War Office. They are, of course, a picked body of clergy with wide experience of soldiers and their difficulties. There are, however, several very strong reasons which have influenced the Bishops in India against such a change. We have always felt it very desirable that our Government Chaplains should regard India as the sphere to which they are to work for the best years of their lives, and, if possible, learn the language so as to be in a position, if called on, to conduct an Indian service for our Christians. Our Government Chaplains have always identified themselves completely with the work of the Diocese, helped in out-stations work and interested many of the military in the missionary work of the Diocese. We have felt that it would be impossible to expect such knowledge and help from Chaplains who are only in India for short periods of service. And now that the Church of India is an independent daughter Church of the Church of England with its own Constitution and Canons and its Synodical Government, it is felt additionally undesirable to have any semblance of separation between our English, military and civilian people, and other kinds of religious work.

The work in our cantonments is too well known to make it necessary for me to describe it. I remember how on one occasion when the Chaplain and his wife were ill and in a very depressed state over the death of a dear child, I transferred them for a fortnight to our small hill station and took temporary charge of the station myself. It was a most pleasant experience. Everybody from the General down was extremely kind, and what with hospital visiting, the soldiers' institute, the social club, my Sunday work including a service for the soldiers' children, watching the soldiers playing football and the officers playing polo, playing tennis and golf, and numerous invitations to messes, the time flew.

A Chaplain in a military station in India has a splendid opportunity of helping men. They respond very quickly to one whom they trust. There is the inevitable temptation to which young men are exposed everywhere. My experience of men leads me to think that there are a small percentage of men to whom what are called the "sins of the flesh" offer but a small temptation, and there is a larger percentage to whom the temptation is almost overpowering, and much the larger who may under strong and good influences run the straight course. The late Lord Kitchener and Bishop Lefroy had several discussions on this question, and at the former's request, Bishop Lefroy wrote a little pamphlet, urging on the highest grounds that men should fight the good fight against impurity and self-indulgence. Shortly after his death I had this pamphlet reprinted with the title, "The Bishop of Calcutta's last message to our soldiers in India."

My wife always took the greatest interest in our soldiers as four of her five brothers were soldiers, three Colonels and one a Brigadier. During the War when we were in Nagpur we generally had, once a week, about twenty-four of the men from Sitabaldi Fort to spend the afternoon and evening with us. India was at that time largely denuded of its regular troops, who were in the war areas, and numbers of garrison battalions with older men were sent out to take their place. I must say the men thoroughly enjoyed themselves, and after various games, golf-croquet, badminton and tennis and even dancing, and a very substantial tea, went back to barracks in a very happy frame of mind. Many of the ladies of the station often came in and helped to entertain them. At that time there was any amount of kindness of this kind shown by the civilian people to our soldiers in India. I cannot forget my children's services in Pachmarhi during the hot weather. I frequently motored up to the soldiers' quarters and brought down a number of the children. On one occasion I packed in over twenty, and I must admit that not long after one of the springs broke!

I have many very pleasant recollections of days I spent in the military stations of my Diocese before and after the War. I still recall very vividly my first visit to Mhow, our Divisional Headquarters, when General Sir O'Moore Creagh, V.C. (popularly known later on as " No More K," when he succeeded Lord Kitchener) was commanding the Division. He had just come back from China and was full of most interesting stories of the leaders of the Allied Forces who had been sent to put things right after the Boxer rising. In those days the 10th Royal Hussars were stationed in Mhow under the command of the late Viscount Byng. I cannot forget the kindness of that distinguished soldier in taking me round the hospital to see his sick men, and what a fatherly interest he clearly took in them all. During subsequent visits to Mhow, generally annual, I was frequently the guest of the General at Flagstaff House. Memory recalls the names of Generals Lloyd Payne, De Voeux, Wallace, Sir C. Kemball, Sir H. Holman, Sir John Shea and Sir R. A. Cassels—the next Commander-in-Chief in India—who with their ladies showed me much kindness.

I specially recall the days when that brilliant soldier, General Stratford Collins, was there. He had passed on to the Northern Command at Rawal Pindi when his career was cut short by cholera, while on a fishing expedition. Mrs. Collins was a great favourite, the soul of kindness and wit. It was said that she was one of the few persons who could chaff Lord Kitchener. On one occasion he got his own back. She was extremely stout and heavy, and in an earthquake in Simla the floor on which she was sleeping gave way, and she was carried in her bed through to the next floor. Everyone congratulated her on her marvellous escape, but when she met Lord Kitchener in the Mall, he simply said, " What is this I hear of you? " When she asked what, he replied, " I hear you put your foot on the floor and went through! " In those days the Rev. Charles Palmer was Chaplain of Mhow, and the soldiers loved his sermons. He preached once on the text, " Beware of dogs " when Mhow was suffering from an epidemic of mad dogs. Another of the Mhow Chaplains was so popular with the Inniskilling Dragoons that when the regiment was transferred to Muttra (that well known pig-sticking centre), the Colonel wrote and asked me if I could not possibly have him transferred to them in the Lucknow Diocese, and it would make their happy family complete! I knew this Chaplain in piping times of peace; I was with him for a time in the hard and trying days of the summer of 1916 in Mesopotamia, I saw him in hospital in Bombay invalided from Mesopotamia and reduced almost to a shadow, and I heard the Matron of that hospital say, " He keeps us all alive by his cheeriness." When he was Chaplain of Mhow a poem was composed about him. Among its verses, and there were a good many amusing ones, three of them ran thus :

> " If you want to know who's who
> Ask the Padre.
>
> If you get into a row
> Tell the Padre.
>
> If you want a friend in need
> There's the Padre."

I can never feel too thankful that when that terrible catastrophe of the Great War broke on the world in 1914, the Diocese of Nagpur was eleven years old and was approaching years of discretion. How could one have attempted to start such a Diocese in war time when all one's thoughts and prayers were concentrated on that one appalling tragedy and on those who were drawn into it? India, as many of us know, was called upon almost at once to send an Army Corps to France under General Sir James Willcocks. One of its Brigades went from Jubbulpore in our Diocese under the command of General Sir H. Fanshawe. Only six or seven weeks before I had been taking long walks and climbs with him in our hills round the Pachmarhi plateau, observing his splendid condition and how he climbed up Chauragarh, our steepest climb, under an Indian sun, without turning a hair. I had remarked casually to someone, " I think the General is in training for a European War! " Little did I then think how close at hand it was. It was a touching sight to see the Jubbulpore Brigade entraining for Bombay late in a winter's night, with many wives weeping and bidding their men farewell. Eight months later I was with them for a short period in France. With them went the Rev. Kenrick C. Horwood as their Chaplain.

In the early days of the War the Church in India supplied as many Government Chaplains as could be spared for active service. Bishop Lefroy was very anxious that the Church should take its part worthily and that every suitable Chaplain should have an opportunity of work in the War areas. As the War went on, however, and our armies grew into hundreds of thousands, it can be easily realised we were unable to supply the large demands even of Mesopotamia and East Africa. It was impossible to deprive a military station of its Chaplain, for when its regular garrison or large portions of it went to the Front, its place was taken by Territorial or Garrison Battalions sent out from England or returned from Mesopotamia. And so, as was only to be expected, the War Office, with the whole of the Church of England to recruit from, took charge of the supply of Chaplains in every war area,

and those Indian Chaplains who were in Mesopotamia and
East Africa came under the principal Chaplains appointed by
the Chaplain General. Reading over my charge to the clergy
of my Diocese at my fifth Visitation after the War, in February
1920, I find the following passage written with war memories
still very vivid : " During the War, as might naturally be
expected, our work had to be carried on under considerable
difficulty. Most of our English clergy wanted to go on active
service with the troops, and a considerable proportion of them
finally went. When reading the names of those who went I
feel it but right to emphasise the fact that the list would have
been considerably larger had the Diocese been able to spare
more. The names of the fortunate ones who actually went
are as follows :

> The Rev. K. C. Horwood, who was with the troops in
> France and Mesopotamia from 1915—16.

> The Rev. P. J. Molony, who was with the troops in
> Mesopotamia from 1916—17.

> The Rev. E. R. Clough, who was with the troops in
> Mesopotamia from 1917—18.

> The Rev. Harvey Staunton, who left Ajmeer in December
> 1917, and died of pneumonia a few weeks later at
> Aziziyeh on the Tigris, when on his way to Head-
> quarters at Baghdad.

> The Rev. Canon Alex Wood, O.B.E., then Head of the
> Scottish Episcopal Mission at Chanda, afterwards
> Bishop of Chota Nagpur, who served with the Indian
> Cavalry for two years, 1916—17, in France, and for
> one year, 1918—19, in Palestine.

> The Rev. R. Hack, who served as Chaplain in France and
> East Africa for a period of fully four years.

> The Rev. N. E. Marshall, who was in Mesopotamia at
> Barra in 1916 and later on for over a year in Perria
> with the East Persian Cirdon Brigade.

> The Rev. A. B. Roberts, who served on the North-West
> Frontier in the Afghan Campaign, 1919—20."

Of those who left us on active service, two returned much
shaken by the climate of Mesopotamia and their strenuous

days out there, and three did not again serve in the Diocese. Harvey Staunton's death came as a great shock to all who knew him, and especially to the staff of the Mayo College at Ajmeer. During the years he was Chaplain of Ajmeer in Rajputana, he had lived with one of the College professors, and as an old Notts county cricketer and Rugby Blue at Cambridge, the sons of the chiefs and nobility in Rajputana in the College whom he often coached, looked on him with much respect.

Shortly after his strenuous days with the Indian Cavalry in France and Palestine, Alex Wood was made Bishop of Chota Nagpur, and only returned to the Central Provinces to succeed me as the second Bishop of Nagpur, when I retired in 1926. His letters to the Diocese when on active service, though closely censored, gave us a most thrilling account of the tremendous and grilling experiences he and his Cavalry Brigade were passing through.

CHAPTER XII

THE WAR. 1914—16

My visit to the Indian Corps in France, 1915—My first visit to the Army in Mesopotamia, 1916.

WHILE I was on leave in England in 1915 for six months, I discussed the question of my relieving one of the Indian Chaplains who were with the Indian Corps in France, for a couple of months. The Chaplain General felt that my short time suggestion was unworkable though he was quite ready to take me on as a Chaplain for the duration of the War, and as I had no intention of resigning my Bishopric, I was more than pleased when, through the kindness of Sir Douglas Haig, I received an invitation to pay a ten days' visit to the Indian Corps, and while there to be the guest of the Corps Commander, General Sir James Willcocks, at his Headquarters at Merville, in Artois. Those were indeed days of deep interest and thrill. Sir James Willcocks and his staff treated me with very great kindness. A Chaplain, the late Rev. Ronald Irwin, D.S.O., M.C., met me at Boulogne and was attached to me during the whole of my visit. He knew everyone and everything about the Corps, and arranged a very full programme of engagements which enabled me to meet a number of the regiments and people I knew in India, and address various bodies of soldiers in all sorts of places. I had arrived on a Saturday evening, and on Sunday morning, after an early Communion, I found myself addressing the Dehra Dun Brigade, whose Brigadier, Sir Claude Jacob, is now a Field Marshal. Our service was held in a school house, and my nephew, Captain Edward Berry, M.C., then Adjutant of the 9th Gurkhas, helped me to get the seats in order. A year later I stood by his grave in Mesopotamia. The afternoon was spent up at the Front and in the evening I preached in the Mairie in Merville. The Hall was crowded, and four Generals sat in one of the front benches. It was St. James's

Day, which gave me a splendid opening for a talk on life and death, the short life and martyr's death of St. James, and the long life of his brother, St. John. I was told that most of my congregation were going up that night into the front trenches, and as I shook hands with all of them as they filed out of the Hall, and they were indeed hearty handshakes, I knew that some of them would in all probability never attend a service again.

Each of the ten days had services and talks arranged for me at some place along the fairly wide front covered by the Corps. I was very fond of opening my address with the question which St. Bernard of Clairvaux used to put to himself when on his various missions : " What doest thou here, Bernard ? " I have always felt that this saying of our Saviour when a boy in the Temple embraces the deepest principle of man's life : " Wist ye not that I must be about my Father's business ? " I tried to make these men of ours realise that as they had left home and all they loved at the call of duty, the call of their King and Country, God would not forsake them in their hour of peril, or suffering, or death. Of course I spoke of the Home over there, and of Christ's great love. I hope I brought comfort to many. One always felt one was talking to dying men. Irwin thought the address with this opening got home, and I hope he was right.

One afternoon we were having a service in an orchard when an enemy aeroplane came scouting over us and we lay low and kept still, for it was probably scouting for the German guns. Another service for the Cavalry of the Corps was held in a field near one of those delightful woods which are dotted about that part of France. One could not help being struck by the wonderful way the fields, not far behind the trenches, were being cultivated by old men and maidens and boys while all the men were fighting, many of them far away. One day I had the great pleasure and honour of lunching with Sir Douglas Haig at Aires. I was deeply impressed by the perfect calm which seemed to possess him and surround him. One might have been lunching with him in Simla or in Scotland during quiet days of peace, instead of in the middle of a tremendous struggle in which such crushing burdens were laid on him. Before I left he very kindly took me into an office and showed me huge maps with the various positions of our forces, and of the Germans. I met him once again shortly before his death when my wife and I lunched with him and Lady Haig at Bemersyde. We had an interesting talk after luncheon. Among many interesting things he showed me in his study was an amusing picture of how the British Generals received Mr. Lloyd George's congratulations after our victory! I also visited my old friend, General Sir H. Fanshawe, who was commanding a Cavalry Division with his headquarters in a charming old French chateau.

Certainly by far the most illuminating and interesting vision of what the War meant was given to me one afternoon when I sat in a dug-out at the top of Mount Kemmel. From there one could see at one's feet a wide stretch of southern Belgium. Ypres was already in a state of ruin as were a number of the small towns and villages in that area. The woods had suffered terribly. Many thousands of soldiers were manning the trenches, but not a man was visible even with powerful glasses. The friend with whom I was sitting and talking in this obscure trench or dug-out was a Major in the Royal Artillery, whom I had last seen in Jubbulpore. He was directing his battery against some German positions not far away from Hill 60. It was indeed a scene of dreadful desolation and misery. Nine years later I visited Kemmel with my wife on our way home from India. It was a beautiful sunny afternoon in May, and when one saw what the Belgians had done in six years to repair the awful ravages of the War and how everywhere they had put the restoration of their Churches as the first thing to be done, one was really filled with admiration at their indomitable spirit.

My days in France passed all too quickly. On the morning of the day I returned to England I had the sad task of burying a very promising young fellow in the Indian Postal Department. He had been to call on me a few days before, as his headquarters in India had been at Ajmeer in Rajputana. He had been making enquiries near the front trenches as to how everyone was getting their letters and parcels, and coming back in a car through a cross road called popularly, " Suicides corner," a German shell killed him and the driver who had both driven me a day or two before to Mount Kemmel. I saw his poor mother and sister in London just after my return. My nephew accompanied me to Boulogne on my return journey. We never met again as he was killed nine months later in Mesopotamia.

When we returned to India in October I settled down to my usual routine of winter work and winter touring, though our thoughts and prayers were with our soldiers, and all our women folk were as busy as they could be in providing things for the Red Cross Society. At that time I had no idea that I should have any chance of visiting the War area again. Early in July 1916, however, I heard from Bishop Lefroy that the late Bishop of Lahore, Dr. Durrant, who had been with the troops in Mesopotamia, and had done such good work in 1915, though most anxious to go again, was forbidden to do so by the doctors. Bishop Lefroy told me that he had suggested my name to the Army Commander in India, and wished to know whether I was willing. Needless to say, I needed no pressing, and after all necessary arrangements had been made with my Archdeacon for the work of the Diocese, and having got my necessary uniform (for I was going on special military duty) I journeyed to Bombay with my wife, and went on board the hospital ship which was to take me to Basra.

No one was allowed to go to the War area without a triple inoculation for cholera, enteric and paratyphoid, and as it had been impossible for me to be inoculated before starting, I received the first half of a triple inoculation going out of Bombay harbour on a rough day in the monsoon. Fortunately I am a good sailor. Like the person who found the Atlantic uninteresting, I cannot say I was attracted by the Persian Gulf. There is nothing romantic about its rocky islands, and, like the Red Sea, it can be unpleasantly hot. I think I rather wondered how I should find the climate of

Mesopotamia, for shortly before I started I had been told when playing golf with a Major who had just returned from there that few people over fifty escaped heat stroke!

On my arrival at Basra I was met by the Principal Chaplain and the Rev. E. O. Jervis, who accompanied me during the next two months all over the War area. Under the advice of the then Army Commander, General Sir Percy Lake, it was decided that I was to proceed as soon as possible to the Headquarters of the Tigris Corps near Kut. As one of my several duties was to hold confirmations, the Army Commander felt that if I spent a fortnight at our most advanced positions where we were in close contact with the Turk whose advanced trenches at Sanayat were within eighty yards of ours, those Chaplains who were further down the river at Sheikh Saad and Amara, would have more time to prepare their candidates.

Before describing my journey up the river to the Corps Headquarters, let me briefly recall what went before the tragedy of Kut, and what immediately followed. Our campaign in Mesopotamia started with a series of brilliant little successes, which lured on our small army further and further until we were in sight of Baghdad. There came our crowning victory at Ctesiphon, when after inflicting heavy losses on the Turks, and capturing many guns and prisoners, General Townshend found himself almost immediately outnumbered by four to one owing to the arrival of fresh Turkish Rediff Divisions, set loose by the evacuation of Gallipoli. That he was able to get away without being annihilated and to get away with his wounded and Turkish prisoners, gives some idea of the fine fighting qualities of this little army of ours and its able leader. About 100 miles south of Baghdad across the desert (though it takes the tortuous Tigris 206 to get from Baghdad to Kut), lies the small town of Kut-el-Amara, two-thirds of which is surrounded by the river. Here our small army, exhausted after severe fighting, made its first halt, and was shut in by a powerful Turkish army, and five months later it was literally starved into surrender. Of the various attempts we made to relieve Kut, I need not write. Had we known that General Townshend could hold out for five months and had he known

RIVER FRONT, KUT-EL-AMARA

KUT-EL-AMARA

that his food supply would last so long, we need not have made our earlier attacks across an open desert against a cleverly entrenched enemy. Our men fought splendidly. In the battle of Beit Aiessa, April 16th to 17th, our last big fight before Kut fell, the Turks alone lost 3,000, and our casualties were very heavy. And when Kut fell it is not hard to understand what the feelings of our Army were. We had made great sacrifices and had failed. When I was starting for Mesopotamia I received a letter from Army Headquarters from a General I know, saying, " The men are naturally depressed, they want cheering." When Kut fell, one of the Chaplains took as his text, " By the waters of Babylon we sat down and wept " ! The position was indeed a most trying one.

The late Sir William Willcocks' description of the climate of Mesopotamia as " fierce " accurately tells us what it is like for much of the year. Fiercely cold in winter and fiercely hot in summer, it is a country which requires the recognised necessities of civilisation to make it bearable. There was our Army, 350 miles from the sea, facing the trials of the hot weather without any of the comforts or relaxations to which our soldiers are accustomed in an Indian cantonment. Adequately to maintain a large body of troops at such a distance from its base when the sole way of transport was up such a winding, tricky and shallow river, ever changing its channels and throwing up mud banks, was an almost impossible task. On came the hot weather with constant dust-storms, plagues of flies, many of them biting ones, and fierce heat, and it came on men weary with fighting, depressed by failure, ill-protected against the fierce rays of the sun, and but poorly fed. The want of green vegetables was responsible for a lot of sickness and scurvy. Fortunately, the nights brought some measure of relief, for the nights near Kut seemed to me to be cooler than in the plains of India. Still, the conditions were appallingly bad; thousands of men went sick; many died; they were evacuating from Mesopotamia when I arrived 20,000 a month sick and wounded. It was a time when no light burden was laid on those in command to keep up the morale of the men and to occasionally fight under such peculiarly trying conditions.

My journey up the river on a P boat with 600 soldiers, mostly Indian, filling every available space, was a novel experience. It took us several days. On our third day one of our gallant little Gurkhas was seized with cholera, and was dead by nightfall; in so crowded a ship isolation was almost impossible. Fortunately, it was our only case, and I was filled with admiration at the marvellous coolness of the young doctor who treated the case, as he was only just qualified and fresh from a London hospital. My small party consisted of my Chaplain, the Rev. E. O. Jervis, two British orderlies and my Indian servant, De Sousa. As De Sousa was our Indian cook, and it was necessary for me to have someone to cook my rations when wandering about the country, my wife had insisted on his going with me. The British orderlies were very fond of him as he cooked their rations also, and he soon became known as Susie. I arrived early on a Monday morning at the Headquarters of the General commanding the Tigris Corps, the late Sir Alexander Cobbe, V.C. From him and his staff I received a very hearty welcome and everything was done to help me in my work.

During the next fortnight I visited nearly every unit in the Corps, holding services on various occasions. The camps were fairly widely scattered and some of them had received strange names. Thorny Nullah was called after a small green thorny shrub, and Twin Canals, where two irrigation channels were close to one another. There were two camps near Sheikh Saad with a hillock and a pool, which were very unpopular, and which a sapper officer named on his map, Sodom and Gomorrah, the Mound of Lot's wife and the Pool of Siloam. This led a young soldier to write to his mother as follows: " Dear Mother. Here we are in the Holy Land. I have seen Sodom and Gomorrah, and the Mound of Lot's wife, and the Pools of Siloam. You will read all about them in the Bible! " I had to consecrate many graves, some in the presence of a large number of their comrades, and the service was always followed by a simple address on the Christians' hope. We were shelled, of course, from time to time, and when the Corps Commander's camp was shelled three times in the week of my arrival, people naturally began to talk about Jonah! One Sunday morning when I was going to an early Communion an aeroplane dropped a bomb unpleasantly close, but I was fortunately uninjured, and the two men who got it were not seriously wounded. On another occasion when going to the camp at Beit Aiessa to bless my nephew's grave and place a little wooden cross upon it, we came in for the latter bit of a bombardment of the camp, and were compelled to leave our car. When later on I was about to hold a service rather near Kut at Ess Sinn, the General of the Division asked Headquarters for an aeroplane which was refused on the ground that I was quite accustomed to bombardments!

It was interesting at the end of a day's outing at the camps to talk with the Corps Commander and hear his views on various matters. Everything was done to keep up the spirits of the Corps. One evening there was a concert, held on the banks of the Tigris by moonlight. The stage was made by two barges on the river. There was an amusing topical song composed for the occasion called " The year two thousand and ten." The song was full of topical and even personal allusions and indicated that the Mesopotamia campaign had nearly a century to run! One afternoon the Cavalry, Royal Artillery and Staff had a jumping competition. It recalled to my mind how, when a German airman saw a football match going on behind the lines in France, he reported that the British soldiers seemed to have gone mad!

We all of us have read the story by Rudyard Kipling of the Regimental Bhistee, or water carrier, and how the soldiers thought he ought to get the V.C. Well, it was indeed a big experience for my cook, De Sousa, to find himself under fire on the second evening after our arrival. I had been out in the desert to bless some graves with a small escort of Indian Cavalry, and had just dismounted from my horse and walked to my tent when the bombardment began. He and I stood side by side while the shells shrieked over and around us, and De Sousa showed no outward sign of fear. One shell killed all the men servants of a Punjab Regiment near us, including the cook, and for the next few days De Sousa cooked their meals until he had taught one of their Syces to cook for them. At this advanced position cooks were not applying for vacant posts!

After saying our farewell to the army near Kut and Sanayat, we went down the river to Sheikh Saad, the advanced base where I was the guest of the 13th Division, the Iron Legion, as it was called from its record at Gallipoli, under General Maude. They had sustained heavy losses at Gallipoli and in Mesopotamia and the staff was rather young, and there were a large number of young recruits among the men. Here I spent a pleasant week without the morning or evening bombardments. The Mess was like a big family, and General Cayley like a wise and kind father. We rode out one or two afternoons to bless graves, and I gave various addresses to different units. One afternoon I spent with the Air Force, and before the service a rather famous airman flew me up to get a view of the Suwaikeh Marsh or lake which the Turks were using to protect their left flank.

My next move was by a P boat with the Staff of the 13th Division to Amara. Everything went splendidly until on reaching a bend in the river we saw to our horror no less than three vessels, stuck in the main channel. Then, in trying to avoid a similar fate, we experienced an even worse one. We lay on a mud-bank in two feet of water between the old channel and the present one, and there we remained for two whole days in spite of all the heroic efforts of our Captain. As our voyage was only supposed to last for twenty-four hours our supply of bread failed, but fortunately my cook "Susie" discovered a bag of flour which my wife had most thoughtfully placed among my stores, and the tea cakes and bread which "Susie" made were pronounced by the staff to be the best they had tasted since they left England. Words but faintly describe our Captain's exertions and sufferings! There he was by the dim light of the false dawn away in his dinghy, searching for a channel of escape. And then at length when we had made up our minds to spend the rest of our lives on this mudbank, and when we had lost all hope and faith in swinging off by anchors, the unexpected happened and we were free.

Amara is certainly one of the pleasantest spots in Mesopotamia, and no place could have been more wisely selected for our advanced hospitals. Here I spent several days visiting the hospitals, holding a confirmation, consecrating its cemetery and holding a Quiet day and conference with the Chaplains. Amongst the Chaplains were Addison, V.C., Dixon of the Lahore Diocese and Fulford who was killed a few months later. One of the subjects discussed at our conference was regarding complaints made in the papers and letters of a shortage of Chaplains in Mesopotamia. I was interested to find that those Chaplains who were best acquainted with the conditions of affairs between Amara and the Tigris Front, expressed their belief that the supply at that time was adequate. This was a matter on which I had been asked to get accurate information by the Metropolitan. While in Amara I was the guest of the Military Governor, a distinguished officer in the Indian Police. His knowledge of Arabic and his intimate knowledge of all that was going on in Amara, including an acquaintance with its strange medley of people, made him a most interesting host. I think the people who impressed me most were the Kurds and the Chaldean boatmen. The Kurds were a fine looking people, uncouth, wild-looking with extraordinary black hats and curious garments. They came from the mountains between Mesopotamia and Persia. They are descendants of the fighting men of Darius, the Mede. The Chaldeans belong racially, I believe, to the fighting races of ancient Assyria. They are fine physically and are Christians.

The strangest of all the people in Amara, though by no means the finest, are the Sabæans. They claim to be descendants of the original disciples of St. John the Baptist, who were driven by persecution into Persia from where they migrated into Mesopotamia. Their religion is an extraordinary mixture of Judaism, Islam, and Persian superstitions with a very faint tincture of Christianity. They cast horoscopes and divinations and are polygamists. When I questioned Zahroon, their chief man, about what the Gospels tell us of St. John the Baptist, he was blankly ignorant of everything beyond the fact that St. John was Elizabeth's son. He knew nothing of

St. John's martyrdom and death. All their services are either by or over running water. Part of their marriage ceremonies take place in the river and any departure from the prescribed ritual is punished. An enormous amount of baptisms take place, which in winter must be responsible for a number of deaths. The Sabæans are famous for their silver work. It is inlaid with black antimony, and some other substance, and is often decidedly curious and quite pretty. Our Army in Mesopotamia must have been an enormous boon to them and their industry. One of the most striking persons in this community was an elderly maiden lady named Kartassa, the sister of Zahroon. She was a veritable Amazon and certainly the most manly figure in the whole crowd. I was told that it was by no means an uncommon thing for women among the Kurds to join the Kurdish Cavalry.

Before leaving Amara I consecrated an extension to its cemetery. Amongst those whose last resting place is in this cemetery is the late Surgeon-Colonel Sir Victor Horsley, whose death at an early age was a terrible loss to the army and nation. I took a really good photograph of his grave at the request of one of his friends to send to his widow. From Amara I returned to Basra for a few days before visiting the Army which was operating up the Euphrates. During my five weeks up the Tigris things had been steadily improving, transport difficulties gradually diminished and the hospitals emptying. There was a pleasant " nip " in the air which told me that the cold weather was approaching. My host in Basra during this visit was Captain A. T. Wilson, D.S.O., Deputy Chief Political Officer in Mesopotamia. Since those days he has been for a time High Commissioner in Mesopotamia, and is now Sir Arnold Wilson, M.P. The Political Mess was a most pleasant one. On the morning after my arrival in Basra I met by appointment the Rev. A. C. E. Jarvis, who had been sent out by the War Office to obtain full information about Chaplains and everything connected with their work in this area. I then learnt for the first time that for the rest of the War all ecclesiastical arrangements in Mesopotamia would be taken over by the Chaplain-General at the War Office, and that while our Indian Ecclesiastical Establishment would be called on to supply a given number of Chaplains, the larger number would be sent from England or Egypt. As I had only recently visited the Tigris Front and Amara, I was able to give Mr. Jarvis pretty full information about that area and make it unnecessary for him to go over the same ground before returning to England. Later on in the week I was extremely glad to hear from General Sir Stanley Maude, who was now in supreme command, of the high opinion he had formed of the Chaplains of his Army. "You will have to live up to a high standard if you go to Mesopotamia," were the actual words of an Indian General to one of the Chaplains of my Diocese who was bound for Mesopotamia.

Now about my visit to Nasariyeh, at that time our most advanced position on the Euphrates. My journey there was to have taken thirty-six hours, but actually it took nearly four days. I had a very pleasant companion on the voyage, Colonel Arthur Brodrick, who commanded the Queen's Territorial Regiment at Nasariyeh. Just as we were starting the Captain of our steamer was taken seriously ill, and another Captain had to be found. Then when we got to Chabesh, near the Hommer Lake, we found that the launch, which had been sent down from Nasariyeh to bring me up, had broken down. Fortunately a dredger which had been brought up from the Irrawaddy was not far away, so on it I took refuge for twenty-four hours. I called it the Hommer Lake Hotel, and when all its engines were going hard the variety of noises were not conducive to sleep. My day on the dredger was enlivened by a visit from an Arab Sheikh, who, hearing that an important Christian Mullah (a Bishop!) was on board, came to beg me to use my influence with the Commander-in-Chief to have the blockade on his villages removed. His people had been very troublesome, sniping at our troops, and the blockade placed on them and the villages as a punishment and deterrent, prevented him from getting coffee and tea and tobacco from Basra. He was a big powerful man. On the third day at about 4 o'clock in the morning by the red light of the false dawn, we started across the Hommer Lake in a large bellum not unlike a big heavy gondola. We were propelled by poles for twenty-four miles, so one can easily realise that it was not a speed boat. The Hommer Lake is the strangest bit of water I have ever seen. For months in the year this vast " bit of a dampness " twenty-four miles in diameter and almost circular, surrounded by marshes, carries a depth of from fourteen to twenty inches. The dredger had been sent up from Burmah to make a channel across the lake, but I do not think it was a great success, for when I visited Nasariyeh six months later, I went there by train across the desert in eight hours. What is this Hommer Lake? How comes such a vast layer of thin water to be spread over so wide an area? The answer seems to be that after running nearly 1,700 miles, the great river Euphrates loses much of its water in this lake. A percentage doubtless escapes into the stretch of water between Chabesh and Qurna, " the Garden of Eden! " and a small portion makes its way to Gurmet Ali, near Basra, where it joins the Shatt-el-Arab, but the vast bulk remains in the lake, a home for wild fowl. It certainly did seem strange to see men walking about unconcernedly with their buffaloes and cows out of sight of land. Night was falling before we reached Akikah, and the Commandant had become anxious and had sent out a boat to search for us. I spent the night at the friendly mess of an Indian regiment, and as it was rather inaccessible for Chaplains, held an evening service before dinner, and an early Celebration of the Holy Communion before leaving in the morning.

The journey up the Euphrates from Akikah to Nasariyeh was very different from my journey up the Tigris. Here one saw trees in abundance, acacia, willow, palm and plenty of cultivation. Numerous villages with broad square watch towers could be seen which reminded one of the familiar towers of village Churches in England. To have a strong, well fortified tower in his village is the ambition of every sheikh.

Nasariyeh is a pretty little town not unlike Amara. It has its arcaded bazaars, and a graceful minaret dominating all its buildings, and like all the riverside towns in Mesopotamia has its bridge of boats. Here I spent four most pleasant days

IN MESOPOTAMIA : 1916

Page 152

as the guest of General Sir Harry Brooking whom I had known when he was chief of the staff at Mhow, Central India. A comfortable room was prepared for me at Staff Head-quarters, which was called "Lambeth Palace." The building was an old Turkish hospital. I had some delightful services especially one for about sixty wounded in a recent battle, one of whom had had a wonderful escape, having been shot through the head. He spoke to me after the service of his great thankfulness to God for having preserved his life.

At Nasariyeh, again through the kindness of the General, I was able to pay a visit to Ur of the Chaldees, the birth-place of Abraham, the Patriarch. It needed some arranging as the desert country round Ur was in a disturbed condition. How-ever, a squadron of Indian Cavalry, a body of Arab Cavalry led by their friendly sheikh, and some Gurkha Rifles, took care that I was neither killed nor caused to be taken away to Baghdad. The Mound of Ur is visible for many miles across the desert. At Ur, before the days of Abraham, stood a temple to the moon god Sin, who gave his name to the peninsula of Sinai. Three thousand years before Christ, Ur of the Chaldees was one of the sea-port towns of the Chaldees, and to-day it is 100 miles from the Persian Gulf. I picked up some sea shells which reminded me of this geological change.

Before leaving Nasariyeh I met an Englishman who had a strange life story. Born in Bristol, he had run away to sea when a lad of sixteen, and after experiences in America and on an island near the Philippines, had become a steward in a P. & O. boat. Then he joined the Aden Police. While in Aden he was seized with the desire for life in the desert, and making his way up the Persian Gulf he joined an Arab tribe and turned Mohammedan. Hearing that his country was at war with Turkey, he made his way to Nasariyeh and gave our Intelligence Department considerable help by his information of the surrounding Arab tribes. He was indeed a mystery man! I sometimes wonder what happened to him after the War, and whether his half-Arab daughter whom he said was to be educated in England has returned to this dweller in tents! I spent a few days in Basra and held two confirmations before returning to India. My return voyage to Bombay was uneventful save for two days on a sand bank at the mouth of the Shatt-el-Arab. On arriving at Bombay I at once proceeded to Jubbulpore to report to Bishop Lefroy on my interview with Mr. Jarvis, regarding the new arrangement for Chaplains in this War area. At Jubbulpore, where my wife met me, I learnt that a dead plague rat had been found in my suit-case which contained my ordinary black clothes, and much to the amusement of everyone save myself I had to appear in uniform till fresh clothes arrived from Nagpur.

CHAPTER XIII

THE WAR

My second visit to the Army in Mesopotamia, 1917

MY second visit to Mesopotamia in the spring of 1917 was in many ways very different from the autumn and early winter of 1916. It was a visit to an army elated with victory. The surrender of Kut in April 1916 had been forgotten in the capture of Baghdad a year later. There was no sense of despondency or disappointment in the atmosphere. True the hospitals were full of wounded men, for there had been very heavy fighting and the casualty list of killed and wounded was a tragically large one.

A little over five months had passed since I was last in Basra, and I soon saw how quickly things had moved during that short period. Everything looked cleaner and even the famous Asher Creek smelt sweeter. The biggest transformation of all, however, was in the roads. Four hundred and seventy miles of new roads over the area covered by Basra and its suburbs of Makina and Margil, was a record of work. Much water-logged land had been reclaimed and the camps were admirably arranged. Then, too, on the river front one saw numerous wharves and jetties with a fine dry dock well on the way to completion. I fully appreciated a friend's casual remark that even if the Turk could push us out, he would be well advised to leave us where we are for two or three years at least, just to let us get things in proper working order. I spent Holy Week and Easter in Basra, holding one large confirmation and a small one in one of the hospitals. It was an imposing sight to see 200 soldiers with Generals and Officers kneeling at the Holy Communion on Easter Day. Two important matters came up for discussion before I left Basra. There were now a number of our Indian Christians in Mesopotamia and the Metropolitan was most anxious that while we were sending Chaplains for our English soldiers we should not neglect these

Indians who were connected with the Army. Three months later the Rev. A. French, an S.P.G. missionary in Bombay, arrived in Mesopotamia accompanied by two Indian clergy, one from the Lahore and the other from the Madras Diocese. The second matter, also one of great importance, was connected with the whole question of the consecration of cemeteries in Mesopotamia. The Army Commander, General Sir Stanley Maude, had sent word to the Base Commandant at Basra to discuss this question with me before I started on my tours. As Bishop Durrant had consecrated cemeteries at Basra, Nasariyeh and Amara as early as 1915, consequent on the number of men killed in battle round these places, and as I had consecrated two more cemeteries at Basra and an extension to the cemetery at Amara during my visit in 1916, and as I had been informed in all cases that the land had been secured either by purchase or gift, and that all the cemeteries which we had consecrated were situated in or near towns where we had every guarantee that they would be properly cared for, I informed the Base Commandant, after some conversation, that I could see no solid ground for objection to the course we had taken. Of course no one would dream of consecrating cemeteries away in the desert, where numbers of our men were buried, as to do so would be but to invite the Bedouin with his vulture-like habits to desecrate them for purposes of loot. To anticipate events which happened later on in this tour, I consecrated no less then eight more cemeteries, and blessed a number of battlefields and graves. One can comfort all who mourn for their dead in Mesopotamia by telling them that the exact position of all these little lonely spots " which are for ever England " are carefully marked down on maps prepared for this purpose by the Graves Registration Committee.

On Easter afternoon, in response to a special invitation from a large number of West Indians connected with the Army Transport, I held a service at their workshop. The singing of their own selected hymns was, as one might have expected, extremely good. Some of them bore very distinguished English names, the relics of their slave owners. On Easter

MY NEPHEW'S DESERT GRAVE : BEIT AIESSA, 1916

CONSECRATION OF OLD CEMETERY : BAGHDAD, 1917

night at the request of the Rev. A. Dixon, the Organising Secretary of the Y.M.C.A. in Mesopotamia, I addressed a gathering of over 700 soldiers at their Palm Garden Branch. I spoke on the future life, a subject so much in everyone's thoughts at that time.

Late on Easter night, again accompanied by the Rev. E. O. Jervis[1] as my Chaplain, we went on board a small steamer called the *Wasp* which was to take us up the Karun river to Ahwaz, near the Anglo-Persian oilfields in Persia. Here, at the request of General Younghusband, I consecrated a cemetery, a piece of ground given by a local Sheikh. We had a very nice parade service in the morning followed by the Holy Communion. On Thursday morning just after daybreak we motored across the desert to Sus, the ancient Shushan. It was a seventy mile run with almost no landmarks save two points on the Kharkeh river. This river is famous for its purity and history tells us that Cyrus always drank bottled Kharkeh water. Sus, or Shushan, the ancient capital of the small warlike state of Elam, and later the southern capital of the Persian monarchs, is beautifully situated in a well watered country with no less than three rivers in its neighbourhood. Twenty or thirty miles away a noble range of mountains, from 10,000 to 12,000 feet high, snow-capped even in April, peered out of the heat haze. Here Æschylus, the Greek poet, laid the scene of his famous play the " Persae," and here Alexander the Great found over eleven millions in gold. Shushan was famous, too, in our biblical history. Here the Jewish patriot and reformer, Nehemiah, lived at the court of Artaxerxes, and from here he journeyed across the desert to Jerusalem on his arduous and perilous mission. It was to Shushan that Ezra was returning from the Holy Land when death met him by the waters of the Tigris. At Shushan you see the tomb of the prophet Daniel. Its pine-apple tower, as Lord Curzon accurately describes it, is more quaint than beautiful. It is now used as a mosque. Needless to say, when resting after breakfast, for our run across the seventy miles of desert had taken little more than three hours, I opened my Bible and read

[1] Mr. Jervis was killed by a tiger two years later near Bangalore.

once more the stories of Esther, Daniel and Nehemiah.

During the afternoon we wandered about the ruins of the Palace of Darius which were most disappointing and not to be compared for an instant with the vast ruins of Babylon. Most of the "great finds" had been sent by the French archæologists to Paris and there was no museum as there is at Babylon to give one any idea of the past. In fact, after wandering about the ruins, and returning to the magnificent building which the French archæologists have erected for their residence and research work, I could not help remarking that if Darius could revisit these scenes he would think that the archæologists' house was finer than his Palace! Our hosts were a few officers of the 23rd Indian Cavalry commanded by the late Major Egerton. We had a little evening service in one of the courtyards of the castle by the light of a single lamp. The hearty singing of our one and only hymn, "Abide with me," in the surrounding darkness, at the conclusion of the service, was most impressive. On my return to Ahwaz, the Chaplain, Mr. Owen, had a number of his soldiers awaiting me for their confirmation. My next Sunday was spent at a convalescent camp at Muhammera, where the Karun river meets the Shatt-el-Arab. Nobody need be surprised that the text of my morning sermon was Nehemiah, Ch. i. v. 1 : "I was in Shushan the palace." In the afternoon I consecrated the old British cemetery at the request of the British Consul. Then came a visit to Nasariyeh, this time by train in only eight hours from Basra. Here I held a confirmation and here I found myself facing three British regiments. The Chaplains said they wanted to give me a picture of a really good parade service as a reward for my visit!

On returning to Basra I made ready for my journey up the Tigris to Baghdad. It was a very different journey from my last one, only seven months before. When I first visited Mesopotamia, in August 1916, there was the strangest assortment of river boats running up and down the Tigris and Euphrates, which one could well imagine. The Indus, Brahmaputra, Ganges, Irrawaddy and Nile sent all sorts of steamers, and even the Thames had sent a number of his small steamers, six of which had foundered (so Lord Hardinge told the House of Lords) on their way out.   Now this Gilbert and Sullivan motley fleet was being replaced by a small fleet of ships built since the War began, with broad beam, but shallow draught, fitted with powerful engines and with modern conveniences, electric light, fans, bath-rooms, etc.   Wonderful to relate, all these modern P boats had made the journey from home under their own steam and only two had failed to reach Basra.   One of the two disappeared on a stormy night in the Bay of Biscay, and the other was lost south of Suez.   I must say that I am lost in admiration for our British sailors, not only for our splendid Navy and Mercantile Marines, but also for the men who risked and lost their lives in cranky cockle shells, tramps, river boats and barges in the Great War.

> " Toll for the brave,
> The brave that are no more."

A few days at Amara, and on April 26th I boarded the steamer for Baghdad.   Just as we went on board we saw six young soldiers fresh from England carried on shore, suffering from heat stroke.   To those who are unaccustomed to a heat which sometimes resembles what is given off by a blast furnace, the heat off the desert is often rather a terrifying experience; you cannot escape from it on the deck of a P boat.   I heard later that all the lads had recovered.

On May 1st I reached Baghdad and learnt on my arrival that I was to be the guest of the Army Commander, General Sir Stanley Maude.   Baghdad is too well known to need much description from my pen.   As one approaches it by river from the south one sees the beautiful golden domes of the Mosque and Shrine of Kazimain, standing up behind it. The Tigris at Baghdad is certainly a very fine river, at its narrowest about 300 yards, and at its broadest about 600 yards.   On both sides stand well built two-storied houses, the most conspicuous at this time being our handsome British Residency.   It is, of course, from a Mohammedan point of view a holy city.   Hither, in the eighth century, the caliphate, or headship of the Moslem religion moved from Damascus, and here the Abbaside Caliphs remained for some centuries till the Caliphate passed to the Mamelukes in Egypt, and later on to the Ottoman Turks. I shall always remember my first meeting with General Maude that afternoon of May 1st. He had been through a winter of fierce battles. His carefully laid plans and daring decisions had brought about brilliant successes. And yet when I congratulated him in his study that afternoon his only remark was on the splendid way his soldiers had fought! Careful plans had been made about what I was to do during the following month by the Army Commander, in consultation with the newly-appointed Principal Chaplain, the Rev. A. C. E. Jarvis, who later on became Chaplain-General at the War Office and is now Archdeacon of Sheffield. To him I owed a great deal during this visit.

On the day after my arrival in Baghdad at the Army Commander's request I conducted the funeral of Lieutenant the Hon. F. I. Thesiger, the Viceroy's oldest son, who had been mortally wounded in action on the Adhain river two days before. He was a gallant boy who, although wounded on two previous occasions, still stayed on fighting with the Army. Another afternoon I attended a reception at the military Governor's, where I met the heads of the various Christian Churches in Baghdad. I was informed that the total number of Christians in the city was rather less than ten thousand, the Mohammedans numbering about ninety thousand and the Jews sixty thousand. After a very pleasant tea I said a few words to them through an interpreter. I dwelt on the pleasure of meeting brother Christians in a land where hitherto Christianity had been despised and persecuted. In view of our divided Christendom (nowhere more apparent than in Baghdad) I urged strongly the duty of praying for the unity of the Christian Church, and of our showing kindness and tolerance to those of our fellow Christians who are not of our own Communion. It really was a unique and interesting gathering as there were present two Armenian Bishops-elect, and the leading Christian clergy of the city. Later on I called on the Armenian Bishop, who told me of the sufferings of his people

at the hands of the Turks. After my interview I was taken
by one of his friends to a large house where a large number
of Armenian women and children were living. They had
been forced to become the mistresses of Turkish soldiers after
their husbands were killed, and now they had been left behind
in Baghdad. It was a sorry spectacle. I was told one day by
an officer that the Turks, after leaving Baghdad, had wired
suggesting a Christian massacre, but the telegraphist, knowing
that the British Army was near the city, sat on the message!

After a busy week in Baghdad I started away for
Samarra, eighty miles to the north, and our most advanced
position at that time. The train in which I travelled was the
first which had run since Khalil Pasha, the Turkish Commander-in-Chief, had fled away north a few weeks before.
When the Turks were defeated at Istabulat, before retreating
to Mosul they did their best to wreck all their locomotives
and to burn all their carriages and trucks. Twelve large
engines of the eighty ton Atlantic type (made in Berlin) and
three constructive engines taking along with them every truck
and carriage, raced away from Baghdad to the rail-head at
Samarra. On arrival, a charge of dynamite was inserted in
the right cylinder and fire-box of each engine, and the station
blown sky-high. Fortunately for us, one of the big engines
came in backwards, and in their haste they destroyed the left
cylinder and left the right intact. Captain Inkson, M.C.
(formerly Loco Superintendent of the G.I.P. Railway) saw this
at a glance and in a wonderfully short time removed the un-
damaged right cylinder and substituted it for one of the
wrecked right cylinders on another engine. Then with admirable skill and with but little of the recognised repairing plant,
he patched up the fire box and got the engine going. It was
in a repaired truck accompanied by a number of young officers
that I travelled from Baghdad to Samarra. This line, I should
add, was at one end of the Baghdad Railway which was to
link Berlin and Constantinople with Mesopotamia.

One of the first persons who greeted me when I
got out of the truck at Samarra was an old Anglo-Indian
pupil of the Bishop Cotton School at Nagpur, Hubert Thoy.

He was a fitter by trade and had been helping to repair the locomotive.   At Samarra I was again the guest of the Corps Commander, that fine soldier, the late General Sir Alexander Cobbe, V.C., so that I was at once amongst friends. Near Samarra, at Istabulat, the Turks had made their last stand on the right bank of the Tigris and from there, after a fierce battle with many casualties, General Cobbe had driven them north to Tekrit.   One of my first duties was to go with a company of Highlanders and some of the senior officers of the staff to hold a solemn service at the battlefield.   I ascended with some of the staff on the ruins of the railway station, and from there offered our prayers asking for the divine blessing on the departed and comfort for their relations.

At this battle the Earl of Suffolk, who commanded one of the battalions, was killed, and General Cobbe was anxious that the spot where he was buried late at night should be found. Fortunately his servant who had been with him for years was standing by when he was buried along with a young officer in a Highland Regiment.   His servant had scratched a large S on the culvert of the Baghdad Railway close to where he was buried.   After a long search we found the grave and I placed on it a rough wooden cross cut out of some packing case wood which a man in his battery had made, and inscribed.   After blessing the grave I removed the cross lest the Arabs should disturb the grave, and sent it to Lady Suffolk. I believe it is now in the Parish Church where she lives.

The senior Chaplain at Samarra was an old friend, the Rev. W. Lachlan Bell, a Lucknow Chaplain, and he was assisted by the Rev. A. Boyse, a C.M.S. missionary at Baghdad.   One of the trying features of life at Samarra in addition to the heat were the " dust devils " which rose suddenly like a water spout and generally made for the nearest camp when people were at their meals!   Samarra was a famous place in the days of old Babylonia.   Close to it, where the battle was fought, was the Median Wall which was in reality a great dam built by Nebuchadnezzar to enable him to flood all the country north of Babylon and protect it from the incursions of the Medes.   In " The Cradle of Mankind," by Dr. Wigram, and

GENERAL SIR B. FANE AND SELF : SAMARRA, 1917

A FAMOUS MOSQUE : BAGHDAD

"The Caliph's last Heritage," by Sir Mark Sykes, we get a most interesting account of all this country. Everyone interested in this part of the world should read them. From the spiral tower near Samarra which Wigram tells us "is the only Ziggurat or Babylonian Temple tower which has not been ruined in the course of centuries," I had an interesting view across the desert of the tomb of the Roman Emperor Julian, the Apostate. Away to the north was the plain of Dur, which the late Sir William Willcocks suggested was the plain of Dura mentioned in the book of Daniel. He thought that the golden image set up on the plain of Dura (Daniel iii. 1) was the image of Nebuchadnezzar himself to commemorate the opening of the wonderful Nahrwan Canal which takes off from the left bank of the Tigris, and which irrigated the country for about 300 miles as far as Kut-el-Amara. A week later I motored across the dry bed of this huge canal on my way to Sindiyeh to visit the 13th Division. General Cobbe's Corps had been too busy fighting the Turks from Baghdad to Samarra to give the Chaplains any opportunity of preparing their candidates for confirmation. After completing my work in Samarra I returned to Baghdad for a few days to the comforts of my "Prophet's Chamber" in the Army Commander's House, and after that spent several days at Sindiyeh on the left bank of the Tigris and at Bakuba on the Diala river with General Sir R. Egerton's Division. I had referred in a letter to India to my Prophet's Chamber, and was rather amused when on my return to India someone asked me in all seriousness: "By the way, who was the Prophet?" At Sindiyeh I was again with my friends of the Iron Legion, and General Cayley and his staff gave me a warm welcome. One morning, leaving my tent at five o'clock, I ran down in a launch to one of the Brigades where I found four of the Chaplains awaiting me with a large congregation. There were about fifty soldier communicants, and after the service I confirmed thirty-six men. The Rev. W. R. F. Addison, V.C. showed me his list of candidates, seventy-three in number, of whom thirty-six formed a part. He told me he had looked forward to presenting all of them for confirmation that morning, but that in the

M

recent battle near the Adhain river, half of them had been killed or wounded. He mentioned that a good many of them were men who had been " hard nuts," and spoke feelingly of the real change which had come over their lives. Another afternoon we had a splendid open-air service on a dry sand-bank in the river with about 1,200 men present. My pulpit was a plateau of sand-bags with a Persian rug thrown over it. On another day I visited a Brigade some miles away in the desert. While at lunch a Turkish prisoner was brought before the General. He was in Arab dress and had been found hiding in a garden not far off. He was a tall, good-looking fellow, not like an ordinary Turk; his home was near Constantinople, and he had been fighting against us in Salonika as well as in Mesopotamia. When the question was put to the prisoner as to whether he was a pure-bred Turk, the General asked the interpreter, a Baghdadi Christian, whether he understood what " pure-bred " meant! The interpreter immediately replied, " Yes, I understand, he eats good bread! " The same interpreter had informed the General and his staff when they first arrived in this neighbourhood that there were " plenty good petticoats " which turned out to mean plenty of good apricots there. Before leaving Sindiyeh I had another large confirmation for candidates prepared by the Rev. E. Teale, M.C. One of the camps was pitched in a plantation of liquorice which grows in profusion from Anatolia to the Persian Gulf. Liquorice factories for squeezing the roots of this plant abound all along this line of country, and immense quantities are exported, especially to America.

On my return to Baghdad I held several confirmations, and among them a confirmation for about twenty Baghdadi Christians of the C.M.S. Mission. They were very nice-looking people, of either Syrian or Armenian descent. They had been prepared by one of the Chaplains, assisted by the leader of the C.M.S. Community, Mr. David Fetto, a Baghdadi chemist who had been a very true and helpful friend to our British prisoners in Baghdad after Kut fell. At breakfast one morning I met the Rev. E. H. Dunkley, who before the War was a missionary in Burmah, and who had till recently been an officer in a Punjab regiment. He told me that some Buddhists in Burmah had expressed grave fears about his taking part in the War as a combatant. They were sure he would have to undergo some thousands of hells for such impiety!

Bakuba, on the Diala, is a little town with nice gardens. Here I spent three days with General Egerton's Division. His Chief of Staff, a brilliant cavalry soldier and now commanding the northern army in India, helped me in every way possible. Owing to an outbreak of diphtheria in one regiment I had to abandon the idea of holding one big confirmation and had to have two or three smaller ones. I have never seen any place which abounded in storks as did Bakuba. They were there in hundreds and paid not the slightest attention to man. Their noises at daybreak were really appallingly like a vast army of corncrakes. My time in Baghdad itself was full of interest. One afternoon I consecrated its two big cemeteries, the old one to the south of the city and the new one near the Cavalry Barracks, where a few months later the great General Sir Stanley Maude was laid to rest. It was always a great pleasure after a busy day to be dining with the Army Commander. He would for a short time unbend, and tell us some of his experiences in Canada, at the Swiss manœuvres, in Egypt and elsewhere. One evening the Russian Liasion Officer, ————, dined with us. He was greatly puzzled at seeing a Bishop in khaki, and when he saw the badges of a Major-General on my shoulder straps he literally gasped!

Shortly after my arrival in Baghdad I said something to General Maude about my desire to see Babylon, eighty miles distant, before returning to India. As the Arabs had been very troublesome in certain areas during the month which necessitated several expeditions, I had abandoned any hope of going there when greatly to my delight on the eve of my departure for India, I learnt that General Dickson, the Chief officer of local supplies (Army Service Corps), was about to visit Hillah close to Babylon to purchase grain for the Army, and the Army Commander had consented to my accompanying him. The story which was current in the Army about my going with this expedition is rather a good one. I was reported to have said, " Think, General, how it will improve my sermons "— and the General told his Staff, " I heard the Bishop preaching next Sunday at a Parade Service, and decided he must go! " We crossed the desert in a fleet of seven Ford motors and an armoured car. At Hillah we were the guests of the Assistant Political Officer, Captain Mackworth Young, the son of a former Lieutenant-Governor of the Punjab. Our first meal was entirely on Arab lines. A whole sheep, minus the eyes, was placed on the table and dates and curds in plenty. Captain Mackworth Young told us that on one occasion when feasting with a distinguished Arab Sheikh, he was offered the eyes of a sheep as a mark of honour. To have simply refused would have been a mark of great discourtesy, but when he remarked " You will pardon me, Sheikh, but I have a rule never to eat eyes on Tuesdays," the Sheikh was quite satisfied! On the following day, while General Dickson was bargaining with the grain-merchants of Hillah over our supplies of grain for the Army in Baghdad, Colonel Wilcox (now Sir William), the Chief Medical Adviser to the Army in Mesopotamia, Colonel Stanley, Red Cross Commissioner, and I spent the whole day exploring the rivers of ancient Babylon. It certainly was one of the great days of one's life. Owing to the magnificent work of Professor Koldewey and his assistants, a work which had been going on for seventeen years without interruption, great portions of the ruins had been cleared, and one could get a fair idea of what the palaces must have been. Those who would care to know what ancient Babylon was like should read " The Excavation at Babylon," by the German Archæologist, Koldewey, translated by Miss Agnes Johns, and Dr. Wigram's " Cradle of Mankind." I took a number of photos in the ruins and a very good one of our famous specialist, Sir William Wilcox, standing by the Lion of Babylon. On our return journey to Baghdad we spent a few hours at the famous Hindiyeh Barrage, the work of two great engineers, Sir W. Wilcox and Sir R. Jackson, which has brought back the water of the Euphrates to Babylon and

Hillah. It was a really fine sight to see the waters of the Euphrates thundering through the thirty-six arches and gates of the big Barrage, and the Euphrates' salmon leaping in the rough water. And now my time for leaving Baghdad for India had arrived. Sunday, June 3rd, was a busy day with several services, morning and evening, and farewells in the afternoon. After my evening service with the Division at the south of Baghdad, I returned in time for my last dinner with the Army Commander and his Staff. I had been his guest for five weeks, and his kindness and sympathy with all I had tried to do, was more than I could have dreamt of. As he came down to the boat which was taking me to my steamer, he said that he hoped I would soon be back with them again. Little did I then think that less than six months later he would have finished his great task on earth, and passed to his great reward. I am concluding this chapter with a reminiscence of General Sir Stanley Maude, which I wrote a few weeks after his death.

A Reminiscence of General Sir Stanley Maude, K.C.B.

The death of Sir Stanley Maude, the great Army Commander in Mesopotamia, has come as a heavy shock to those who at all realise what he meant to our Army out there. For General Maude was one of the " discoveries " of this great war. The War Office doubtless knew that he was a fine soldier, but even there his real greatness cannot have been fully realised. It needed a big thing like this present war to bring it fully to light.

War is a great " discoverer." Like the Day of Judgment, it brings to light the hidden things of darkness in men and nations, and it brings them out impartially and remorselessly. Is there any weakness in the individual or the nation, out it is sure to come in war. Everything is then tested and strained to the utmost. Some men break hopelessly in the process and some nations like Russia go to pieces.

Some men, however, are discovered by war, and amongst the comparatively few, whose names will be household words for many a long day in our Empire, is the late Sir Stanley Maude. For to him was given the glory of taking away the reproach which had unfortunately attached itself to the British army in Mesopotamia, and of turning what to some looked like defeat into brilliant victory.

No one who had been with the sick and weary troops in Mesopotamia in the summer of 1916, and had seen them again in 1917, could ever think of minimising the quite extraordinary change which had passed over them within six months; and this change we owe to one great man, the late Army Commander. Others will write in due course and with special knowledge of his military genius and of the many fights our army fought and won under his leadership. My aim is but to recall some of the memories which the days I spent with him last summer in Baghdad have left behind— memories which will never fade. I do so because few, at any rate in India, know anything of him, save that he was a great and successful General.

My first meeting with General Maude was in August 1916, when things were very much at a standstill as far as active military operations were concerned. The weather was still very hot and trying and the sickness amongst our troops appalling. General Maude had been spending the greater part of this hot weather in his tent and dug-out, commanding the 13th Division, which lay in front of the Turkish position at Sanayat, eighteen miles below Kut. He had just been appointed Army Commander in Mesopotamia and had come down to Basra to take over command of the Army from General Sir Percy Lake.

On my first Sunday in Mesopotamia I had the privilege of ministering to these two Generals as they knelt side by side at our early Eucharist. A short conversation after the Service, and I left the following day for work amongst the troops round about Kut. Shortly before returning to India in October I had the pleasure of again meeting him by invitation at luncheon and talking to him for some time afterwards about the work of the Chaplains. Little did I dream as I said good-bye and wished him all success in his difficult task

LIEUT.-GENERAL SIR F. STANLEY MAUDE, K.C.B.

Page 168

of the great things which, under his leadership, our army would accomplish within the next few months.

Our next meeting was in Baghdad, just six months later. Sitting in his study working away at his dispatch I found him one afternoon early in May. We talked of what had happened since our last meeting, and the burden of all he said was that with men who had fought like the men of his army anything was possible.

Then for five weeks, living under his roof and meeting him every day, save during those intervals which I spent with the troops at Samarra, Bakuba and Sindiyeh, my acquaintance quietly grew into what I hoped would be a life-long friendship. The house we lived in on the banks of the Tigris was the same house in which the great German strategist, Von der Goltz, had lived for a time and in which he had died.

Life was decidedly on the strenuous side at Army Headquarters, but in the Army Commander's house there was no rush, no fuss, the atmosphere was absolutely quiet and still. The day began early and ended early. Breakfast was at seven, luncheon at one and dinner at half-past seven. The Army Commander rose very early and retired before ten. He never seemed in a hurry, but was always working at full, steady pressure. There were his many and daily interviews with those responsible for various departments of the Army, his conferences with his Generals and staff, his afternoon rides, his visits to the various Divisions; but, though always hard at work, there was never the least sign of rush. It was always quiet strength—very quiet and very strong.

And this leads me to say a few words about some of the marked features of his character as I saw it during those days. No one could have lived with Sir Stanley Maude without seeing that self-discipline was stamped into his very soul. The great General was practically a total abstainer and never smoked. Endowed with splendid health and strength, he certainly never allowed self-indulgence of any kind to weaken his remarkable powers. To me he always seemed the same, never over-burdened by his big responsibilities or anxieties; calm and confident about the issues of war. If he was disap-

pointed, as he well might have been, at the failure of the
Russians to co-operate with him when the Turks were retreating from Baghdad, he took his disappointment with extraordinary composure.   His was essentially a quiet and
immensely strong nature.   And the main root of this great
strength lay, one cannot doubt it, in the region of his higher
beliefs about God and duty.   For never did a Sunday dawn
but the Army Commander was to be seen kneeling in silent
worship at the Eucharist.   It was from this divine spring his
soul drank of those streams which kept it so strong, so pure, so
fresh and so inspiring.

A writer in one of our Anglo-Indian papers has spoken of his
deep reserve, and doubtless to the world generally he passed
as a reserved man.   But to those who were about him constantly, this certainly was not the case.   On many an evening
as we sat at dinner, he would tell us of his days in Canada as
Military Secretary to the late Lord Minto, or of bits of African
campaigning, or of early days in Egypt.   He had commanded
a Brigade of our " contemptible army " and fought at Mons
and had been in the retreat on Paris, when he was wounded.

He had afterwards commanded the " Iron Legion " in
Gallipoli, and but few know that he was almost the last person
to leave it.   It was a dark and stormy night, and the evacuation was almost completed, when, owing to some mistake, the
launch, which was to have taken him off with his staff, was
not at the place of rendezvous.   For nearly three miles he and
the staff had to walk or scramble in the dark along the beach
and cliffs to the nearest landing stage.   Little did the Turks
realise how easily the future conqueror of Baghdad might have
fallen into their hands that night.

No one could have read the letters which I have received
from various persons in Mesopotamia since his death without
realising that, above and beyond the profound admiration
which men had for General Maude's military genius, there
was the real affection which all who knew him had for him as
a man.   Strict and even severe in his self-discipline and in
what he expected of others, he was most kind and thoughtful
for his soldiers.   Over and over again he would break into his

afternoon rides to visit a hospital and see how the men were getting on. If he loved fighting—and there was no one who loved a hard fight better than General Maude—there was not a trace of anything savage or brutal or cruel about his nature. His was, indeed, the soul of a true knight—noble, courteous, chivalrous—" Sans peur et sans reproche! "

And in the very zenith of his powers, when a still greater future seemed clearly in store for him, and when but few of the honours which would have been his had come to him, it was the good pleasure of his God to call him to Himself. Doubtless he had finished his special task—a very big and heavy one in this great world-struggle, and other hands able and strong were ready to guard and increase all he had won for us.

And now, all that is mortal of our great soldier—the Conqueror of Baghdad—rests in the self-same soil as hundreds of our gallant soldiers who, under his leadership, have added imperishable glory to our Army and Empire. And in the years to come the children of our Empire will be told of the great soldier who, like a second Wolfe, passed away in the hour of his triumph at Baghdad.

I have been reading again the " Character of the Happy Warrior " as I have penned these few words. How truly many of its lines describe for us literally this great Army Commander :

> " Who comprehends his trust, and to the same
> Keeps faithful with a singleness of aim ;
> But who, if he be called upon to face
> Some awful moment to which heaven has joined
> Great issues, good or bad for human kind,
> Is happy as a lover."

For General Maude was assuredly one of the Poet Wordsworth's " Happy Warriors "—

> " Whom every man in arms would wish to be."

January 4th, 1918.

CHAPTER XIV

THE WAR AND AFTER

Kashmir—Spanish Influenza in India, 1918—My third visit to
Mesopotamia, 1919.

My wife and I spent the spring and early summer of 1918 in
Kashmir. My two visits to Mesopotamia in 1916 and 1917
had been rather strenuous. I fancy there are few places in
the world which can do a tired man more good than the Vale
of Kashmir. We went there after Easter, when the valley
was looking wonderfully beautiful. The wild flowers, especially
the purple irises, were a great joy. The snowy peaks of the
Pir Panjal and the majestic Haramukh looking down on this
great long valley with the river Jhelum running down it on its
way to the sun-stricken plains of India, are sights which once
seen linger on for ever in the memory. For the first few weeks
of our rest cure we lived in a house-boat fairly near to the
British Residency, where the war telegrams were posted
every day. It was the time when our Army in France was
facing the great German offensive in 1918, " with their backs
to the wall," and all our thoughts and prayers were constantly
in France. Then, when it was clear that the German offensive
had failed, we started off on tours up those two beautiful side
valleys, the Liddar and Sinde. We did a certain amount of
walking and climbing at the head of the Liddar Valley, and
then went up the Sinde to Sonamarg and Baltal. By this time
our legs were in fine walking order, and we were ready for a
rather big effort, a visit to Amarnath, that famous place of
Hindu pilgrimage.

Amarnath is a huge cave in the side of a mountain
at an elevation of 12,800 feet. The cave has a very
high and wide opening, and up against its back wall is a large
ice stalagmite, which resembles the emblem of Shiva, fed by
some subterranean spring. At a certain season of the year
when the sun strikes on this white ice block, come pilgrims
from all parts of India to have their " darshan " or vision of

PILGRIMS APPROACHING THE CAVE OF IMMORTALITY, AMARNATH, KASHMIR

Page 177

the god Mahadeo. Numbers of them lose their lives from exposure, for it is a long, high and exhausting climb. We got on to the snow shortly after three o'clock in the morning, and did not reach the cave till eleven o'clock, an eight hours' trek without food. Along the high and narrow valley which we had to ascend, we were for some miles walking over frozen snow with a river running beneath us. These " snow bridges," as they are called, are often 100 feet deep. When the sun, in May and the following months, becomes powerful, these bridges sag in the centre and fall into the river. When nearing Amarnath, and walking at the upper side of a snow bridge whose centre had given way, my feet suddenly went from under me and I found myself rapidly gliding downwards, with my wife, who had endeavoured to save me, holding me by my collar. Fortunately, my alpenstock was a powerful one, and though lying down I succeeded in driving it into the frozen snow, and so saving us. It was rather a jar, as had we gone into the river, we would have been carried under a snow bridge for a mile ! Our coolies, who were carrying our food, were very alarmed ! On the following day we were in such excellent training that we did the climb up to the head of the Zogi La, the pass which leads into Western Tibet. Our companions on this trek were Mr. and Mrs. Charles Farquhar and their Airedale. Mr. Farquhar was at that time Inspector General of Police in the Punjab. The scenery was wild and beautiful. More than twenty years before I had crossed the Jelap La, 15,000 feet, into Eastern Tibet as far as the Chumbi valley, the early part of the route taken by the Mount Everest climbers. On that occasion our party consisted of my old friend, Richard Greer of the Bengal Civil Service, and the late Sir Edward Henry, Chief Commissioner of London Police. The view of Kinchinganga, 28,600 feet, the second or third highest mountain in the world, from the head of Jelap La, baffles description. Its mighty precipices and huge glaciers present a picture immense and almost terrifying, and yet for a time one would like to have been one of the great eagles which was soaring around to whom heights and depths meant nothing !

The winter of 1918 was a very sad one for India. While everyone was rejoicing that the War was over, and thanksgiving services were being held all over the country in Churches, Mosques and Temples, India was just emerging from one of the most terrible epidemics that had ever visited the country. The " Spanish influenza," as it was called, which had visited the armies in Europe, had floated across the world to India, and had carried off, it is believed, six million of its people. The death roll in the Central Provinces alone amounted to 800,000. Many of the villages in our remote jungles lost nearly all their adult population, and the condition of the survivors, especially the small children, was too piteous to describe. The British officials worked as they always did, day and night, to bring help to these much-affected people. My wife and Mrs. Frank Prideaux, the wife of one of our leading judges, undertook special work at Nagpur Hospital, and received special thanks for their services.

The War had left us with a heavy legacy of a reduced staff and shortened finance, and I had begun to forget my two visits to Mesopotamia when I was again called upon to go there in September 1919. There were still a number of our troops scattered all over the country, especially north of Baghdad and in Persia, and the Chaplains were ready with a number of men for confirmation. Within a week before starting I received a welcome telegram from General Sir George MacMunn, the Army Commander, who had always been a most kind and helpful friend during my former visits, permitting my wife to accompany me. The voyage was smooth and pleasant. Our fellow passengers included a travelling Opera company who were going out to enliven the war-weary garrisons. Their director happened to be a Mr. Bishop, which naturally led to amusing remarks about the Bishop arriving in Mesopotamia with his Opera company! After a couple of days at Basra, where I held a confirmation, we went straight up the Tigris to Kut, in a comfortable vessel, a stern wheeler from the Irrawaddy. As we passed the battlefields of Sanayat, Beit Aiessa, and where the river bends round Kut, one's thoughts went back to those days of tremendous fightings with sad losses, and constant suffering and hardship, through which our gallant troops, under General Maude, with his two splendid Corps Commanders, General Sir William Marshall and General Sir Alexander Cobbe, V.C., had passed before victory had crowned their efforts. Kut was, of course, intensely interesting. It had a special interest to my wife as her youngest brother, now Brigadier Arthur Brodie Haig, M.C., had been one of its ill-fated garrison, which was starved into surrender after a five months' siege. I should add that my brother-in-law, with seven other brother officers who were taken prisoners when Kut fell, made a wonderful escape three years later from Yozgad in Asia Minor. The story of this escape is told by two of the party in " Four hundred and fifty miles to freedom." On our return journey I consecrated its cemetery at the back of the town close to the trenches in which all had fought and many died. We went by train across the desert from Kut to Baghdad, and received a very warm welcome from General MacMunn and his staff.

Our time in Baghdad, in addition to confirmations and services, had one experience of peculiar interest which is well worth the telling.

Forty miles from Baghdad towards the Persian frontier at Bakuba on the Diala river there was at that time a refugee camp of Assyrian Christians. We spent one day in visiting this camp escorted by a young political officer, Mr. Reid, who had at one time been a missionary of the Archbishop of Canterbury's Assyrian Mission in Kurdistan. This is how I described the visit to my Diocese in India when writing in the October 1919 Magazine : " Imagine a camp with 3,500 E.P. tents and with a population of from forty to forty-five thousand refugee Assyrians, men and women, and children. These Assyrian people, all of whom are Christians, were compelled more than a year ago to fly for their lives from the relentless Turk, who was bent on their extermination. Many of them came from Kurdistan, that mountainous country which lies to the north of Mosul, and others came from the country around Lake Urumiyah. Pursued by the Turk, and protected partly by their fighting men and partly by a body of British Cavalry sent up by General Sir W. Marshall, they had trekked into Persia and from there into Mesopotamia, a good many hundred miles, where they found themselves under the protection of our Army. It certainly was a tremendous task to have to provide for this huge family at such short notice. They had arrived in a terribly distressed and diseased condition. 3,000 children had died on the journey, and there were 13,000 children still alive in this vast camp. These refugees were drawn from various Churches, as well as various localities. Among them were Nestorians, in whom our Church is especially interested (owing to the work of the Archbishop of Canterbury's Assyrian Mission), Gregorians, Armenians, Syrians and Chaldeans. One must remember that these Assyrians had been our allies during the War. They had joined in with the Russian Army as it advanced on Erzeroum. When, however, Bolshevism disintegrated the Russian Army, these Assyrian and Armenian allies of ours were left high and dry to face the Turk alone." On all that has befallen them since then I must not dwell. I can but recall the glad reception we met wherever we went in that huge camp. I still have photographs taken when we were surrounded by a cheery crowd of these people, and when I was sitting between two Metropolitans! The women in the camp, mistaking my wife's pendant pince-nez for a sacred emblem, kissed it most reverently! We were entertained at lunch with great kindness by the Camp Commandant, Colonel Cunliffe Owen, and his wife; and met, later on, a friend of mine, Colonel Lloyd, I.M.S., the principal Medical Officer, and some of his large staff of doctors and nursing sisters. I do not think I ever admired my country more than I did that day when I saw how splendidly we had cared for these people who had come to us in their distress. Would that our Government, before surrendering our Mesopotamian Mandate, had taken the same care for the future of those unfortunate people, as our Army did in those early days!

When the Army Commander had wired to me to India he had stated that my wife might accompany me to Baghdad,

WITH ASSYRIAN BISHOPS : BAKUBA, 1919

WITH CHAPLAINS : BAGHDAD, 1919

but no further! As, however, the country was quiet and he saw that she was not at all nervous, he said she might accompany me to Mosul and Persia. The country between Baghdad and Mosul, which is over 200 miles to the north, is largely desert and very uninteresting. Time was when it had several cities and towns of great importance which to-day have no interest save to the archæologist. Shergat, then the rail-head, was our first and only halt between Baghdad and Mosul. Here was the site of the ancient city of Asshur, whose god Asshur gave his name to the city and to that warlike race. I had an interesting confirmation at Shergat of Burmese Christians, with an admirable Burmese interpreter. We spent the night in the camp of an Indian regiment, whose Colonel and officers made us most welcome. On our way to Mosul we passed another ruined city, Caleh, the ancient Nimrud, which we visited a few days later. Mosul lies on the right bank of the Tigris with the ruined city of Nineveh on the left bank. There are some interesting old churches in Mosul, and our garrison was allowed the use of one of them by the Jacobite Bishop. Nineveh was to me a great disappointment. The great winged statues in the British Museum had led me to expect something as great as one had seen in Baalbec and Babylon, but whatever there may be of interest in Nineveh is still buried under the ground. I really think my wife saw much more in Mosul than I did, for while I was busy one morning she was taken for a fly over the surrounding country by an officer in the Royal Air Force. Two things impressed me about this rather quaint city; its splendid background of Kurdish mountains, and its most unpleasant, if healthy, sulphurous atmosphere.

From Baghdad we went to Persia. One can hardly imagine a greater contrast between two countries lying side by side than between Mesopotamia and Persia. For Mesopotamia is nothing better than a low-lying desert from which the sea has obviously receded. Were it not for its two great fertilising rivers, the Tigris and the Euphrates, one can hardly imagine any human being wanting to live in it. Without these rivers it would be simply a Sahara. And yet what a history it has had! For in very early days it was the home of one of the earliest of human civilisations, the Chaldean, with magnificent systems of irrigation which made it a most fertile country; and in later days it was the centre of the Mohammedan religions till Hulagu, the Hun, smashed its irrigation systems and made the country a waste from which it has never really recovered. Certainly if Mesopotamia was at one time the world's greatest monument to what man can do in building up, it is also a living example of what man can do in breaking down, and the physical contrast of Mesopotamia to Persia is most marked.

Almost at once as one approaches the Persian frontier one begins to ascend one of the several passes which link it with its low-lying neighbour. During a motor run of over 500 miles from the frontier at Kuraitu to Teheran we were frequently moving at elevations of 7,000 feet, and crossing passes up to 10,000 feet. Its great ranges of mountains, running from north-west to south-east, struck one as being singularly bare of trees and vegetation (Persia wants water badly), while the colours of these rocky mountains towards sunset were singularly beautiful. At this time a number of British and Indian Troops were dotted about the country as far as the Caspian, and I had work to do, confirmations and consecration of cemeteries at several places. At Kermanshah, Hamadan, the ancient Ecbatana, and Kasvin, we made our halts, and, of course, we stopped for an hour to take photos of the famous rock sculptures at Behistun, 300 feet up on the cliff of a mountain, which an early traveller thought were the figures of our Lord and His Apostles, but which Sir Henry Rawlinson correctly interpreted as representing Darius the Great receiving homage from subject kings!

At Teheran we spent five delightful days at the British Legation as guests of Sir Percy Cox, then British Minister to Persia. Teheran is really a beautiful city at an elevation of little more than 4,000 feet. Behind it stretch for hundreds of miles the Elburz mountains with the huge cone of Demavend towering 19,000 feet above everything. Our stay with Sir Percy Cox was peculiarly interesting because at this time Persia was passing through a peculiar phase of its history.

Its ancient glory had departed, its Shah had abdicated, it was in danger of being overrun by Bolshevist Russia, and in its difficulties it had turned to England. For a short period, helped by its strong belief in the wisdom of Sir Percy Cox, there was every indication of an Anglo-Persian *entente* in which England might be called upon to take over big responsibilities in Persia for a generation till Persia had got on its feet, and during which period young Englishmen might find interesting work in its civil administration as well as in all other departments of state. As we now know, these Anglo-Persian conversations never got beyond the range of preliminary discussions, but none the less, at this period, it seemed likely that they would really mature.

Society in Teheran was decidedly cosmopolitan. There were Russian officers attached to the North Persian Cossack Brigade, and Swedish officers connected with the Gendarmerie of Central Persia, while British Officers with Indian Cavalry kept order in south Persia. We had a beautiful service in Teheran on All Saints' Day made additionally solemn by the losses which some of the leading people there had sustained in the War. Of course I visited the American Presbyterian Mission in Teheran, and at Dr. Jordan's request addressed the boys in his college. We were accompanied on our tour by the Rev. R. E. G. Newman, M.C., who acted as my Chaplain. We found him most pleasant and helpful. On our return journey we halted in Baghdad for a few days before going back to India. Here we had the pleasure of meeting at dinner, Miss Gertrude Bell, that distinguished traveller whom I had met during my previous visits. She certainly gave her life to Mesopotamia, and one is glad to think that her memory is being enshrined in Baghdad in the museum which bears her name. Two years before, in May 1917, I had confirmed over twenty Arabic-speaking Christians connected with the C.M.S. Mission, who were of either Syrian or Armenian descent. Again I was asked to confirm a dozen more of this Community and again Mr. David Fetto acted as my interpreter. Years have passed since I heard of Mr. David Fetto and his family who had been such good friends of our people throughout the War

N

and afterwards, and I am sure that no Chaplain of ours who was in Baghdad will ever forget their goodness and kindness. On our way down the river to Basra, through the kindness of the Army Commander, our steamer halted at Beit Aiessa to enable us to visit the battlefield where on April 16th, 1916, my eldest nephew, Captain Edward Fleetwood Berry, M.C., was killed. Everywhere we saw evidence of that terrible fight in which hundreds of brave men were killed. Knowing nothing of modern infernal machines, my wife quite innocently picked up a bomb which had not exploded. Her act, very fortunately, was seen by the British officer who was with us, and the bomb was placed back on the ground very carefully. There in the middle of that battlefield was an Arab encampment with the children playing about and the cattle grazing where they could. It brought back to memory Southey's famous poem " After Blenheim."

> " But what they fought each other for
> I could not well make out.
> But everybody said, quoth he,
> That 'twas a famous victory."

Again through Sir George MacMunn's kind arrangement we spent a morning at Abbadan on our way from Basra to join our steamer at the Persian Gulf. Here in tanks which are connected with the Anglo-Persian oilfields by large pipes, 200 miles long, there are always one hundred million gallons of crude oil, and every day two millions are refined. At one time the Baktiari tribesmen used to amuse themselves with cutting these pipes, but when their chieftains were given shares in the Anglo-Persian Oil Company this was very quickly stopped. Our voyage to India in the British India troopship was without event till the last day, when, owing to rather heavy seas, many of the 700 Indian troops suffered from what they described as the " Chakkars," that horrible feeling of giddiness which precedes the indescribable. So ended my third and last visit to the Land of the Two Rivers.

CHAPTER XV

I FEEL I must say a few words about these English Church Schools of ours in India. When I first arrived in India early in 1892, I was soon led to realise the importance of the education of the children of the European and Anglo-Indian Community. In Hazaribagh which was the headquarters of our Dublin University Mission, I was asked, in addition to my missionary duties, to act as English Chaplain to the residents in the station, and to those English and Anglo-Indian people who were scattered about a district as big as Wales. I found that all the children, most of whom were members of our Church, were receiving their education in the Roman Catholic Convent where they were taught by French nuns. It seemed to me just as much, if not more, the duty of our Church to care for the education of our own children as it is to open schools for Hindus and Mohammedans. I placed my views before the Committee of the Dublin University Mission with the result that two ladies were sent out from home to undertake this work. We opened our little school and the nuns closed theirs which was no longer needed.

We have three large Church Schools in the Diocese of Nagpur, one at Nagpur and two at Jubbulpore. We are educating in these schools about 700 children. There are also in the Diocese a number of railway schools, where the European and Anglo-Indian children whose fathers are in railway service are receiving an English and Christian education. Many of these railway schools take part in our annual examinations in religious knowledge conducted by one of our senior clergy.

As I have recently written a small book on our English Church Schools in India, it is unnecessary for me to do more than to single out certain points connected with them which everyone interested in India and in the spread of the Gospel out there ought to know. Our Church of India, Burmah and

Ceylon has to maintain seventy-five English Church Schools in India and Burmah, where about 14,000 children are being educated. Fifteen of these schools are in the hills, eight are in plateau country and the remainder are in large centres of European and Anglo-Indian life. Some of the schools have histories which go back more than two centuries to the days of the East India Company. A number of these belong to Bishop Cotton's period just after the Mutiny. Large sums of money have been raised in India at various times for the starting and maintenance of these schools. These domiciled European and Anglo-Indian children of ours must receive an English and Christian education. They cannot attend Hindu or Mohammedan schools, nor can they attend the ordinary Zillah or Government schools, where their teachers would be Hindus or Mohammedans, and the teaching would be in the different vernaculars of India, and without any religion. Nor do we wish to hand over our children to the various foreign Roman Catholic brotherhoods and sisterhoods (French, German, Italian, Belgian, Irish and Spanish), who would almost certainly teach them to disbelieve our form of the Christian faith, and would have no interest in maintaining their loyalty to England, and the British traditions of their ancestors. We feel that these children are our own, and it is our solemn duty to give them the best education we can to fit them for their life in India. These schools of ours are in no sense racial. They are based on English culture and the Christian faith. So highly are they valued by many of the Indian gentry, Christian and non-Christian, that all schools receiving Government grants are asked and expected to admit a percentage of Indian boys and girls varying from 15 to 25 per cent. I should add that eight of our most important girls' schools are maintained by English Church Sisterhoods. Just now owing to political and economic changes in India when many Anglo-Indian fathers are out of work, the difficulty of maintaining these schools is increasing. It may interest my readers to know that two years ago the parents' fees for these schools amounted to over £107,000, the Government grants to £57,000, the endowments to £12,800, and in addition to this a sum of over £25,000 was needed from Dioceses or other sources to keep them up to the necessary standard of efficiency required by Government. That some considerable financial help will be needed from England before long is increasingly evident to our Bishops in India. The late Bishop Montgomery, when Secretary of the Society for the Propagation of the Gospel, asked the Church of India to prepare a full memorandum on these English Church Schools with a view to his appealing for a large sum to help them. The memorandum was prepared largely by the then Bishop of Bombay, the Right Rev. E. J. Palmer, D.D. Before, however, the appeal could be framed on the basis of this memorandum, the European War had broken out, and the War years, followed by years of greatly straitened finance, led to the whole subject being lost sight of. Now, however, in view of the great political changes impending in India, the question of the education of the Anglo-Indian community is coming up with renewed insistence. The future of this community is bound up with the maintenance of these schools. As educated men and women in the new India they may prove of great value to the land of their birth, and to the Church of their baptism. If uneducated, they will sink lower and lower and be a constant reproach to the good name of England, and a serious hindrance to the spread of our Christian faith in India.

During his recent visit to England, the Very Rev. Dr. Graham, who has done such a unique work for the Anglo-Indian Community in his St. Andrew's Colonial Homes at Kalimpong in the Himalayas, came to see me on this subject. His important lecture before the Royal Society of Arts on the education of the Anglo-Indian child has been published in the January and April issues of our Indian Church Aid Quarterly Magazine. Dr. Graham urges us to use every influence to impress on English people, especially our own Church people, the vital necessity of maintaining our schools for this community. He told me that during the past thirty-five years the number of Anglo-Indian boys and girls on these school rolls has been six hundred. These children have been, in many cases, taken from the slums of our great Indian cities, and from worthless homes. A large percentage have turned out splendidly and are filling responsible posts in India, and in the Colonies. When asked by me how he had been able to finance such a large institution he made it clear that the needs of this community, and the past services of their ancestors in building up British India, had specially touched the heart of Scotland and Scottish merchants. His committee had raised during those years £160,000 for their buildings, land and various things for the education, agricultural and industrial training of the children, and they had also raised, as an endowment, about £200,000!

During his visit to India in the winter of 1921—2 His Royal Highness the Prince of Wales addressed a message to the domiciled community on February 22nd: " You may be confident that Great Britain and the Empire will not forget your community who are so united in their devotion to the King Emperor, and who gave such unmistakable token of attachment to the Empire by their great sacrifice in the War." No one who knows the life story of the Anglo-Indian community will ever deny that in times past they have been treated very badly by the country to whom they owe their existence. Instead of being encouraged, they have been ignored and too often despised. When years ago Bishop Potter of New York was visiting Calcutta and staying with the Oxford Mission, he was so deeply touched by the miserable condition of many of this Community in the slums of that great city that he is reported to have said, " If ever the British lose India they will deserve to because of the shameful way they have neglected their own poor people."

There is one country and one Church which could and should right the great wrong which has been done to the descendants of the pioneers of our race in India, and that is England and our Church. The opportunity is now being presented to us. While it is still ours let us not lose it. If one noble Scot can do for a number of this community what Dr. Graham has done, and is doing, what cannot our Church do if it will only rouse itself to action?

CHAPTER XVI

MY LAST YEARS. 1920—26

The Lambeth Conference—Visions of Union and the South Indian Movement—Delegations from Missionary Societies—The Healing Mission —The Mission of Help—Discussions on Self-government in the Church of India—Our War Memorial—All Saints' Children's Home—My History of the Church of England in India—A Tour in the Bombay Diocese— The Blind Maulvie, 1892 and 1923—Farewell to India.

NINETEEN hundred and twenty was the year of the sixth Lambeth Conference, and my wife and I were among a great company of Bishops and their wives who came from overseas to attend it. We were reminded of the Great War by the fact that instead of travelling in a comfortable P. & O. steamer, we had to make the voyage in a rather inferior German vessel, the *König Frederick August,* which had been taken over by our Government to compensate the P. & O. for its many losses. She was built, we were told, to steam sixteen knots for a South American run, but our firemen could only get nine knots out of her, and the day after leaving Malta she went on fire in her coal bunker. When the fire was discovered a number of soldiers whom we were bringing home from Egypt and Palestine helped the firemen for the first day to get at the root of the mischief, and when a number of them began to suffer from the fumes, the majority of our able-bodied first-class passengers took a hand in the work. The ship's bar did a fine trade for the next day or two, as it was very thirsty work down in the hold. Fortunately, the fire was kept sufficiently under to enable us to make Gibraltar without leaving the ship; and there we had to stay for five whole days while all the Indian coal which had spontaneously combusted was removed and fresh coal was put on board.

The sixth Lambeth Conference of 1920 was in every respect a memorable one. It was attended by 255 Anglican Bishops from all over the world. It was presided over, as in 1908, by Archbishop Davidson, whose singular power and winning personality pervaded the whole Assembly. How deeply he and Mrs. Davidson were loved was manifested before the end of the Conference, not only by the handsome presentations made to them both, but by the words of those who presented our gifts. Christendom had been rent asunder by a terrible and savage war. There were those who thought and said that had Christendom been united in one Holy Catholic Church this war could have been prevented. How natural, then, that the biggest questions which came up for consideration at the Lambeth Conference centred round the thoughts of union and reunion. Forth from this Conference went a wonderful appeal for the reunion of Christendom. Those who did not read that appeal years ago might well do so to-day. It was no mere repetition of what is generally described as the Lambeth Quadrilateral, in which our Anglican Bishops had already stated four fundamental principles which in their judgment must underlie any real organic union between the divided Churches. This wonderful appeal embodied a great vision of a united Church in which along with an agreement on these fundamental principles, there would be found rich contributions of spiritual thought and practice now scattered loosely in various bodies of separated Christians. It was an invitation to all Christian bodies to come together and share their riches of spiritual life and work in one great Church and Divine family of God. Can such a noble vision become a reality? This question of unity which was filling the minds of all Christian people at that time was a specially pressing one in India. For some time previously a movement to unite various Christian bodies in South India had been going on. The Anglican Church in South India did not start the movement, but as it developed they were invited to share in it and felt drawn to do so. The Episcopal Synod selected certain of its Bishops and of the clergy to take part in these union conferences. Those selected were men with special knowledge of Church history and theology, and were of different schools of thought. As I was not one of those who took part in these conferences, I can only touch on a few points which impressed themselves on me from the reports we received from time to time. It was abundantly clear that all who took part in these conferences were convinced that to really win India for Christ, a united Church was of vital importance. It was our Lord's will that His followers should be one, that the world may believe that the Father had sent Him. Nowhere in the world did religion divide man from man more than it did in India. Between the Hindu and Mohammedan there ever lay a deep-rooted antagonism ready to burst forth into deadly conflict when anything occurred to affect their different religions. Amongst the Hindus the whole of society was one endless division into castes which would, and could, have no dealings one with another. And now God's great revelation of Himself as the All Holy, All Loving Father of humanity was being proclaimed in India by the followers of His Blessed Son. He was bidding the peoples of India to come to Him and enter into His Church, the family of God. Surely the members of the Divine family should be united through love of their Master to have love and fellowship with one another. The tasks which our delegates had to undertake at these early union conferences were immensely delicate and difficult. Certainly they were most fortunate in having one so specially gifted as Edwin James Palmer, then Bishop of Bombay, to take a leading part in their counsels.

There was at the very outset the question of the Apostolic Ministry as understood by us Anglicans, of Bishops, Priests and Deacons. Some would clearly have liked a Church without Bishops. One venerable old missionary is reported to have said: "He that taketh a Bishop into his bosom taketh a scorpion!" Was it not wonderful, then, that as the days went on and the discussions became more intimate, Bishops became quite popular, and there soon was complete agreement that whatever else they had or had not in the Church of South India, they must have Bishops?

Well, years have passed, since that historic appeal went forth from Lambeth in 1920; conferences almost every year have met in South India to discuss questions and problems connected with this union; another Lambeth Conference in 1930 has again discussed aspects and difficulties, and the end is not yet. There are

well known, able and devout churchmen in India and elsewhere who view this movement with deep anxiety, and there
are, I fancy, a much larger number who view it with great
enthusiasm. It is certainly a great experiment to meet a great
need, and if it proves successful on episcopal lines, and a
genuine union of these Christian bodies with the Catholic and
Apostolic ministry emerges, and does not lead to divisions
elsewhere, it will be a great blessing in India, and a guide
towards union in other parts of the world. Surely it is in
the mission field, if anywhere, that we should expect the
beginnings of the union of Christendom; for is there not
something of a promise in the Benedictus : " That when giving
light to those that sit in darkness and in the shadow of death,
our Lord will guide our feet into the way of peace."

When we returned to India after the Lambeth Conference
in the winter of 1920 we found the atmosphere charged with
a most unfriendly political agitation. On my arrival in
Bombay I had gone up to Surat, " the Cradle of the British
in India," as it is called, to verify certain facts connected with
a history of our Church at which I was working. Imagine
what my feelings were when arriving there at one o'clock in
the morning, and trying in vain to get a cup of warm tea, I
was cheered by the station master with the news that they had
just passed a vote of condolence with Mrs. McSweeny, whose
husband, the Mayor of Cork, had just starved himself to death
in Cork Jail ! The Christmas of 1920 in Nagpur was not as
quiet as our Christmases generally were. The National Congress led by Mahatma Gandhi and the two Mohammedan
brothers, Mahomet and Shaukat Ali, was holding its annual
meeting in Nagpur. Forty thousand political agitators might
be of small account in a vast city like London, but in a town
of 150,000 they looked very large. My wife and I were
introduced to the Mahatma and we had some conversation
with Mahomet and Shaukat Ali. They all seemed very pleased
with themselves and they certainly succeeded in making the
people amongst whom we had hitherto lived in peace and
amity, regard us " with greetings where no kindness was."
One's car would be pelted with stones and mud by small boys

as one went through the villages, and loud shouts of
" Mahatma Ki Jal," " Victory to the Mahatma Gandhi,"
were heard constantly.   Passing away, however, from such
matters which were more disappointing to us than anything
else because we felt sure that the really intelligent Indians
knew we were their true friends, let me turn to some of the
events of real interest to our Church during these my last few
years in India.

Now that the road to India was open we had quite a
number of important visitors from England.   First to come
were delegates from the Church Missionary Society and the
Society for the Propagation of the Gospel.   I have already
alluded to the visit of the C.M.S. delegates, which left us with
very heavy hearts.   Our few C.M.S. missionaries who remained were living almost under the sentence of death for a
long time and it really seemed as if the chief light of the
Church of England missionary work in this part of India
would have to be put out for lack of funds.   Fortunately, the
worst has not happened and I hope may never happen ; for
to have Jubbulpore without a single English missionary
clergyman would be, in my opinion, a fatal mistake, and
forfeit the confidence of many of our English congregations in
the wisdom of those who direct the policy of that great and
honoured Missionary Society.   The delegation of the S.P.G.
to our Diocese had no such unpleasant tasks to perform.
Their only Mission is a small one in Ajmeer.   They looked
into things and promised to report what they had been shown
to their Standing Committee on their return to England.   We
specially invited their attention to the Bishop Cotton School
at Nagpur, and to the Christ Church Boys' and Girls' Schools
at Jubbulpore, and since then the venerable Society has not,
I am glad to say, forgotten them.

Then came another visitor from England, whose visit
aroused deep interest in India and Ceylon.   The late Mr.
James Moore Hickson, of the Christian Healing Mission,
visited our Diocese in March 1921, and held missions in
Jubbulpore, Nagpur and Amraoti.   At all three places his
reputation had gone before him, and he must have been asked

to lay hands on between 8,000 and 9,000 persons in five days. I attended his services in Jubbulpore and Nagpur and at my request very interesting reports of all these services were written by those of our clergy, Chaplains and missionaries who took part in them. No one who was present at these services when hundreds of Indians, Christians, Hindus and Moslems, were holding out their hands in appeal to this man whom they believed to be endowed with a Divine gift of healing, could have failed to have been deeply impressed. When I gazed on that great mass of Indian suffering I could not help recalling the remark of an Indian civilian friend who said, " What India wants is proper medical treatment and sanitation far more than Home rule ! " In some of the reports which reached me one read of remarkable cures, like those in the Gospels, the dumb speaking, the lame walking and even cases of blind seeing. One case which I was shown in Jubbulpore of a blind man recovering his sight almost immediately was peculiarly interesting. To my enquiry he replied he could now see " three quarters," an answer which reminded me of the man in the Gospels who in the early stages of his cure saw " men as trees walking."

I did not find Mr. Hickson, like some faith-healers, decry doctors or medicine, nor did he find any place for the illusions of Christian Science which endeavour to deny the reality of human suffering. What he did believe was that God had endowed him and others with a gift to bring healing and comfort to many whom medical science failed to reach. While he was staying with us in Nagpur, a Mohammedan Nawab, or Prince, came half across India from Gujerat to see him. I gave Mr. Hickson permission to have his interview with this interesting man in my Chapel. A few days later I received a beautiful little pair of silver candlesticks from the Nawab for having allowed them the use of my Chapel. Mr. Hickson was a fine robust and manly person with a real sense of humour, but with a tremendous sense of his gift and vocation. He told me that when in Ireland, a Roman Catholic Bishop had said to him, " If you come over to us we'll make you a cardinal ! " I cannot say that I thought his addresses or his books covered completely or satisfactorily the causes of pain and suffering in the world or even in man, but I believe he had a real gift, and was used by God to bring comfort to large numbers of sick bodies and sick souls.

Our next cold weather visitors were a band of missioners, twenty-five clergy and six ladies, who came in the winter of 1922 at the unanimous request of the Provincial Assembly which had met in Calcutta in February 1920. Their visit is always described as the visit of the Mission of Help to India. They were commissioned by the Archbishop of Canterbury for this great and solemn task at a special service of dismissal held in Westminster Abbey on October 5th, 1922. The way had been prepared for them the winter before by three pioneer missioners, the late Father D. Jenks, the Rev. Courtenay West, and the Rev. Geoffrey C. Lunt, now Bishop of Ripon. The purpose of the visit of these pioneers was twofold; viz. to explain what the Mission of Help actually meant, and to learn the conditions of work and the special types of Europeans and Anglo-Indians there were in each Diocese, with a view to understanding what sort of missioners should be sent. These pioneer missioners had come both to teach and learn. They held Quiet Days in Jubbulpore and Nagpur followed by conferences with the clergy and Church workers. Father Jenks stayed with us at Bishop's Lodge, Nagpur, and won all our hearts. A year later the Mission of Help arrived in India. Amongst them were the Bishop of Peterborough, Dr. Woods, the Dean of Manchester, Dr. Gough McCormick, Canon J. J. Stockley of Lichfield, the Rev. Guy Vernon Smith, now Bishop of Willesden. Some were specially assigned to the Nagpur Diocese, amongst whom were Canon Neville Lovett, now Bishop of Portsmouth, Canon Greaves, now Chancellor of Lincoln, the Rev. Priestly Swain, now Bishop of Burnley, Father Waggett, S.S.J.E., the Rev. Edward Hertslet, now Canon of Bristol and Rector of St. Mary's, Redcliffe, the Rev. Spencer Elliott, the Rev. Reginald Palmer and Rev. E. Southam. Three of the six lady missioners visited our Diocese, viz. Miss Higson, Miss Cowlin and Lady Fletcher. The missioners were everywhere welcomed. I endeavoured to visit nearly every station in the Diocese while the missioners were there. Our Missions in the garrison stations of Mhow, Jubbulpore, Nasirabad and Neemuch were held before Christmas so as not to interfere with the training of the troops. From the Commander in Chief, Lord Rawlinson, down to the Generals of Divisions and Brigades, and the Colonels of British regiments, everyone helped. The missioners in our two biggest military stations were Canon Greaves, the Rev. Reginald Palmer and Miss Higson. All three were speakers with exceptional gifts and no one was more eagerly listened to both by men and women than was our lady missioner, Miss Higson.

It is impossible in a few sentences to describe the missions which were held in many parts of my widespread Diocese during this cold weather of 1922—23. I can still recall quite vividly just a few impressions which are worth the recording. We had quite a large gathering of civilians and political officers one evening at the Indore Club to hear Father Waggett speak on the causes of materialism and its decline. I have seldom heard a more brilliant and convincing address, and I remember saying to a leading civilian as we went away that Father Waggett must have convinced most of his audience that these perishable bodies of ours are in such a state of perpetual flux that the only really permanent things in existence are God and the soul. Canon Lovett's Mission at Nagpur in which he was ably assisted by the Rev. Edward Hertslet was immensely helpful. He seemed to thoroughly understand the people he was addressing. Canon Elliott's addresses to the Anglo-Indians were also greatly valued, as were the evening discussions held in the Circuit House, Jubbulpore, on the "Faith in relation to modern doubt," and "Our modern social life" conducted by the Rev. Priestly Swain. I have already alluded to the great value of Miss Higson's addresses, and in a very quiet way Miss Cowlin did an immense amount of solid good.

The question is always raised after a mission, what permanent good has it done? It would be hard to fully estimate the amount of good done by the Mission of Help to

India because people come and go so quickly out there. That the interest aroused at the time was surprisingly great and that certain study and prayer circles grew out of it is unquestionable. Of the value of one bit of work done by the Mission I can speak with certainty. At my invitation Lady Fletcher took a very long and fatiguing journey from another part of India to address our women at Nagpur and at Mhow. Her visit to Nagpur was well worth while as out of it grew the Wives' Fellowship which still carries on its valuable work after thirteen years. Where I do feel, however, that the Mission of Help has not come up to our expectations is in the comparatively little help they have given the Church of India since they left it thirteen years ago. Perhaps they are not altogether to be blamed for this. They were all very busy people and the claims and needs around them in England are so great that it is fatally easy to forget these people of ours amongst whom they moved for only one short winter. I remember how when I welcomed the first two missioners in Jubbulpore, I said by a happy or unhappy slip of the tongue : " You come to us as a Mission of Hope." I went on to add : " I am sure you will tell the people at home of our needs, the needs of their own people in India." Would that one could truly say that they had done so. Some have helped us nobly and some seem to have forgotten that they ever went to India on a mission of help to their own people.

During the years which lay between 1921 and 1926 the biggest question by far which the Church in India had to face was the question of its connection with the State. Once it had been made clear to us that the Act of Uniformity applied to the Church in India as much as it did in England, and that our Diocesan and Provincial Councils were merely debating societies which could not legislate for the Church, we saw that we were faced with a big and very difficult decision. How could our Church in India grow if it had no independent power within itself to make provision for its own peculiar needs, but had to be tied and bound by customs and traditions formed in England to suit England's needs. Surely, for example, a Prayer Book framed in England over 250 years before, which needed much revision and many additions to meet the needs of the Church in England to-day, could hardly be expected to meet the spiritual needs of a Church like ours in India with its many races, some of whom, like our Indian aborigines, are quite primitive. Had the Church in India, with its rapidly increasing Indian membership, to be tied for ever to the Mother Church of England whose own freedom was in many ways hampered by its connection with the State? Again, the Government of India under the Chelmsford Montague Reforms was destined to become more and more Indian, and its leading officials would no longer be Christian Englishmen, but Hindus and Mohammedans. How undignified and impossible it would be for our Church to have to get the consent, before, let us say, starting a new diocese or consecrating a new Bishop, from a practically non-Christian Government. And if, as a Bridge Church, we endeavoured to bring about union with other Christian bodies, we were fully aware that no other Christian body in India would consent to a union with a State Church. The fact became clear as the leaders of our Church in India faced it, that the legal " painter " which connected Calcutta with Canterbury must be severed, though the golden spiritual " painter " must be made stronger than ever.

To describe the debates and controversies spread over the years between 1920 and 1927, when the legal severance took place by the passing of the Indian Church Act in Parliament without a division would need a volume of considerable size. It was discussed in our Diocesan Councils and Provincial Councils, as well as in special conferences and meetings. In my Diocese the " diehards " regarded our severing our legal connection with the Church of England and the British Parliament as sheer folly. They pointed out that the main support of our Church in India came from the English and that if we took this step we should lose this. When the question came up for a decision at our Diocesan Council for the first time, the voting showed a deadlock, and although as Chairman I had the casting vote which would have turned the scales, I refused to exercise it as I felt that with opinion so divided on this subject it would do more harm than good to force it through. After a visit from the Metropolitan and further discussions, certain facts emerged which largely changed the feelings of those who had opposed the measure.

The main facts which brought about the change were, I believe, that the leaders of church opinion in England, more especially the late Archbishop of Canterbury, for whom our people had an unbounded respect, had made it clear that they approved of this legal change; that the Secretary of State for India had declared in a dispatch to the Viceroy that if the change took place he intended to " maintain unaffected his existing power and obligations in respect to the appointment of chaplains," and the great missionary societies were fully in favour of it. During the years while these discussions were taking place and before the final decision was taken, a strong committee of Bishops and their assessors were preparing with immense care the Constitution and Canons for the future Church of the Province of India, Burmah and Ceylon. These were especially busy years for the Metropolitan of India, the Bishops of Bombay and Madras, and for Canon Western, then Head of the Cambridge Mission at Delhi, and now Bishop of Tinnevelly. Certainly the Church of India can never forget all she owed during this period of her life history to Edwin James Palmer, Bishop of Bombay. Not only in the framing of the Constitution, but also in his discussions in England with the Secretary of State for India, with the Archbishop of Canterbury, and with leading churchmen in Parliament, he played so important a part that one high official at the India Office said to me, he really did not think that the many initial and subsequent difficulties they had to meet would have been overcome, and our India Church have secured its legal independence, but for Bishop Palmer.

Two events of real interest took place in Nagpur during 1922 which link themselves with the memory of a dear friend, the late Sir Frank Sly, Governor of the Central Provinces, which certainly deserve some mention.

On Sunday, August 6th, Sir Frank Sly unveiled the War

o

Memorial to members of the British Community of the
Central Provinces who had fought and died in the Great War.
The service was a most impressive one and was attended by
the General of the Division, Major-General Clery, Colonel
Commandant O'Dowda, units from the Bedfordshire and
Hertfordshire Regiment, the Royal Field Artillery at Kamptee,
the Nagpur Volunteer Rifles, the Boy Scouts and Girl Guides.
The Memorial consisted of a very fine window, by Messrs.
Powell, symbolising "Victory through Struggle, Suffering
and Self-Sacrifice." On one side St. Michael's War with the
rebel Angels in Heaven; on the other, St. George's fight with
the dragon; in the centre our Lord's supreme sacrifice on the
Cross; and above all the figure in Glory of the Victorious
Saviour. Underneath was a very fine tablet of Rajputana
marble executed at Jaipur, Rajputana, on which the names of
our fallen friends were inscribed. Above was carved the Star
of India in gold with its famous motto "Heaven's Light Our
Guide." Below were the pathetic lines:

> " In trench and field and many seas we lie,
> We who in dying shall not ever die
> If only you in honour of the slain
> Shall surely see we did not die in vain."

Few could have remained unmoved when the whole large
congregation, amongst whom were some Hindus and Mohammedans, solemnly standing at attention, heard the Last Post
followed by the Reveille played by the band of the Beds. and
Herts.

Then, on November 9th, the new building for the All
Saints' Children's Home was formally opened by Sir Frank
Sly. It had cost about £4,000, and Government had given
the Hill Crest bungalow, adjoining it, as the residence for the
lady in charge and the Cathedral worker. It was a source of
great happiness to us that we had been able to build such a
fine and suitable Home for the children, near the Cathedral,
and near the Bishop Cotton School where they received their
education. Nagpur had now its small Cathedral Close, with
the Cathedral, Cathedral House, the Cathedral Hall, and the

All Saints' Children's Home within the boundaries of one large compound.

It was on this occasion my wife was awarded the Kaiser-i-Hind Medal for her public work, especially in connection with the National Indian Association and the Girl Guides. The National Indian Association aimed at drawing together Indian and English Society in social ways, and was quite a success in Nagpur. Shortly before I retired, when Sir Montague Butler was Governor, I was also awarded the Gold Kaiser-i-Hind Medal, a pleasant memorial of my days in India. I suppose it is unusual for both husband and wife to receive this honour, and when presenting it, the Governor remarked, " The Bishop has achieved what few of us can, he has got even with his wife."

In 1924 the S.P.C.K. published my " History of the Church of England in India since the early days of the East India Company." It had filled most of my leisure hours for the last seven years. When I first suggested to Bishop Lefroy the need of such a book in view of the widespread ignorance amongst church-people both in England and India, as to what our Church had done and was doing in India, my idea was that each Bishop should write a history of his own Diocese, and that we should bring them together in one volume. When, however, the question was discussed in Synod, the feeling was unanimous that it would be better to leave it in the hands of one person, and I was asked to undertake it. There were others I knew who had far more qualifications than I had for the task, but they had neither the time nor inclination to take it on. Of course everyone helped me most generously and I was supplied with a library of books and pamphlets from all over India. Amongst a number of press notices and reviews which appeared at the time of its publication was a very full article in the July number of " Theology," by Sir Verney Lovett, Reader of Indian History at Oxford. His concluding words I must admit gave me real pleasure : " Perhaps the supreme value of this book is that by bringing us close to men of great faith and power, enabling us to see them walk the earth, and to hear them speak, it leads the reader to aspire to possess at least a small portion of their spirit." Certainly no one can read the lives of Henry Martyn, Reginald Heber, Daniel Wilson, Robert Milman, G. E. L. Cotton, Valpy French, George Lefroy, Pennell of the Afghan frontier, to mention but a few names of a great and goodly company of men and women who gave their lives for India, without feeling some longing to follow in their steps. For the Indian Church has given us such a number of saintly lives that we might well form a new calendar as full of inspiration to the young men and women of to-day, as were the lives of the primitive and mediæval saints to earlier periods of the Christian Church. I cannot forget also that I received a letter from a young gunner officer whom I had met during the War in Mesopotamia to whom I sent a copy of the History at his ordination. When writing to thank me he told me it had already given him material for two sermons!

In the spring of 1923 I paid a three weeks' visit to the neighbouring Diocese of Bombay. Bishop Palmer, who was at that time on leave in England recovering from a severe illness, had asked me to hold a confirmation tour in his Diocese before the hot weather. During this tour I confirmed nearly 600 persons and ordained two deacons and one priest in St. Thomas' Cathedral, Bombay, on March 18th. Of course I visited that splendid S.P.G. Mission at Ahmednagar and had a wonderful confirmation in the beautiful Church of Panch Howds at Poona, where the Cowley Fathers and Wantage Sisters are doing a great work. My interest and admiration was, I remember, specially stirred at Hubli by what I saw of the S.P.G. Criminal Settlement. It was a wonderful revelation of the power of the Gospel and the ability and devotion of our missionaries to see 2,000 vagrant criminal tribes-people living within a large enclosure and gradually being brought under the discipline of a civilised and Christian life. To a remark of mine that the work amongst such a people must be somewhat depressing came the eager reply from one of the workers, " depressing it certainly is not, it is so full of hope." Amongst those whom I confirmed at Hubli was a young fellow who belonged to the " deer-stalking tribe," whose activities were not confined to poaching, and whose temptations were strongest after the sun had set! During this tour I managed to find time to spend a day at Golden Goa, which is beautifully situated up an estuary about eight miles from the sea. What it was in the days of its greatness is well known to many. Now its beautiful churches and monastic buildings are almost deserted. I ate my mid-day meal of sandwiches in the room of a huge convent which was built for 400 nuns! I managed to take a really good photograph of the interior of the Church of Bom Jesu, where the remains of the great St. Francis Xavier are exposed in a handsome glass case at times of pilgrimages. As I wandered round this almost deserted place I was met by a venerable canon, who said to me, " You look very pale, come and have a glass of wine."

Let me conclude this bundle of memories with the story of an event which linked my earliest and my latest days in India closely together. Early in 1892, shortly after my arrival in India, I visited the Cambridge Mission at Delhi with a brother missionary of the Dublin University Mission. Our Mission to Chota Nagpur was then starting its new brotherhood life in India and we wished to see how the Cambridge Brotherhood lived and worked. It was on this occasion, just on the eve of our leaving, that I witnessed that remarkable scene in the Bickersteth Hall at Delhi, where the blind Maulvie on the eve of his baptism had announced his intention of confessing Christ before a large gathering of his Mohammedan co-religionists. The story of that night, which will ever remain in my memory, was told very fully in an account of it I wrote years ago which appears in Bishop Montgomery's " Life of Bishop Lefroy." It was a night of acute spiritual agony to Lefroy and his brother missionaries, for in the middle of his speech the blind Maulvie, terrorised by angry crowds of Mohammedans, broke utterly down and was carried in triumph to a neighbouring mosque. Months later he returned to Lefroy in bitter sorrow, and after a long period in Lahore was baptised. It was in one of the winters shortly before I retired from India that I was summoned to Delhi to take confirmations owing to the illness of the late Bishop Durrant of Lahore.

I had just had an interesting confirmation for the Indian congregation and was leaving the Church when my attention was called to the figure of a blind man standing by himself outside the Church waiting for me. It was the blind Maulvie whom I had last seen over thirty years before on that memorable night. I had just confirmed his son. In a moment he had thrown his arms around me and was reminding me almost passionately of the men of the Mission whom he had loved and honoured : Lefroy, Allnut, Carlyon, Kelley and Wright. They were heroes of this strange old man and their names are linked with my first and most treasured memories of India.

Shortly after Easter 1926 our time had come to say farewell to India. More than thirty-four years had passed since I first landed in Calcutta on January 12th, 1892. I felt that the time had come when for every reason it was better to hand over the work to someone younger and better able to stand the fatigue of long journeyings than I could expect to do much longer.

Farewells are always attended with some sadness and regrets. Our friends in Nagpur and the Diocese generally had given us many proofs of their friendship. Beautiful and touching addresses in English, Hindi and Marathi had been given to us and are now among our treasured possessions, and the Cathedral congregation, specially, had given us two really beautiful gifts. And then came the last farewell at Nagpur Railway Station, not the same station at which I had alighted twenty-three years before, but a fine modern building situated near Fort Sitabaldi.

Everyone who has served in India must recall scenes such as the one in which we took our part that day. Most of those, not absent from Nagpur at the time, whom we had known so well for years (English, Anglo-Indian and Indian) were there to give us God-speed, after the kindly Indian fashion. There were the leading members of the Cathedral congregation, our Indian clergy with Tamil and Marathi Christians, our friends of the United Free Church Mission of Scotland, and even our kind friend Monsignor Coppel, Roman Catholic Bishop of Nagpur. And finally, as heavily decked with garlands (another kindly Indian custom), I was about to enter the train which was to take us to Bombay, I found my legs firmly grasped by my " Boy " Saoji, who had accompanied us everywhere and who was lying prostrate on the platform! It was India speaking to England—" Do not leave us."

INDEX

INDEX

PRINTED IN GREAT BRITAIN BY
THE FAITH PRESS, LTD., LEIGHTON BUZZARD